Start Your Own

CONSTRUCTION AND CONTRACTING BUSINESS

Additional titles in *Entrepreneur's* **Startup Series**

Start Your Own

Bar or Club

Bed & Breakfast

Business on eBay

Business Support Service

Car Wash

Child Care Service

Cleaning Service

Clothing Store

Coin-Operated Laundry

Consulting

Crafts Business

e-Business

e-Learning Business

Event Planning Business

Executive Recruiting Service

Freight Brokerage Business

Gift Basket Service

Growing and Selling Herbs and Herbal
    Products

Home Inspection Service

Information Consultant Business

Law Practice

Lawn Care or Landscaping Business

Mail Order Business

Medical Claims Billing Service

Personal Concierge Service

Personal Training Business

Pet-Sitting Business

Restaurant and Five Other Food Businesses

Retail Business and More

Self-Publishing Business

Seminar Production Business

Specialty Travel & Tour Business

Staffing Service

Vending Business

Wedding Consultant Business

Wholesale Distribution Business

Entrepreneur MAGAZINE'S

startup

Start Your Own

CONSTRUCTION AND CONTRACTING BUSINESS

Your Step-by-Step Guide to Success

Entrepreneur Press and Gregg Kuehn

Ep
Entrepreneur
Press

Editorial Director: Jere L. Calmes
Managing Editor: Marla Markman
Cover Design: Beth Hansen-Winter
Production and Composition: Eliot House Productions

This publication is designed to provide accurate and authoritative information in regard to the subject matter covered. It is sold with the understanding that the publisher is not engaged in rendering legal, accounting or other professional services. If legal advice or other expert assistance is required, the services of a competent professional person should be sought.

Library of Congress Cataloging-in-Publication Data

ISBN-13: 978-1-59918-123-3 (alk. paper)
ISBN-10: 1-59918-123-1 (alk. paper)

Printed in United States
12 11 10 09 08 07   10 9 8 7 6 5 4 3 2

Contents

Chapter 6
Budgets and Estimates: Financial
Techniques for Profitability

Chapter 7
Contribution Margin: The Key to
Understanding Profits

Chapter 8
Promoting Your Services

Preface

There's an old story about the men who drive up to a residential property in an unmarked rusty van, knock on the front door and inform the homeowner that they can reseal his cracked asphalt driveway at only a little more than half the going rate. The homeowner, Mr. Jones, strapped for cash after taking his family on a theme-park vacation, readily agrees to pay cash for the work. The next day, three men arrive bright and early, sweep dirt and leaves off the driveway, and proceed to apply a thin black substance to the driveway. They finish the job quickly and place protective yellow ribbon around the driveway.

After packing their tools in their van, they show Mr. Jones the finished project, telling him not to walk or drive on the asphalt for two days in order to give the sealer plenty of time to harden. "You don't wanna track the black stuff into your house," they inform him.

Delighted to have saved money and have the job finished quickly, Mr. Jones readily pays cash for the job. He's so happy with the results, he forgets to get a receipt. The only thing he knows is that the lead man's name is "Joe."

Very early the next morning, while Mr. Jones is dreaming about his golf game scheduled for that day, a wild and thunderous rainstorm awakens him and his wife. Trees bend in the storm, small branches break, and their rain gutters overflow. They give up their sleep and plod to the kitchen for their morning coffee.

Mr. Jones steps outside as dawn is breaking to retrieve the morning newspaper that is usually tossed onto his driveway. He takes a few steps and is dumbstruck by what he sees. His driveway is no longer black. The old cracks are still evident and even more prominent because of the rain. But his lawn is black and the gutter along the street is full of black goo. The light bulb goes on as Mr. Jones realizes that he has been taken. The men did not seal his driveway yesterday—they just "painted" it with some sort of black liquid.

Weeks later, after paying more than the going rate for a proper sealing job and additional money to have a portion of his lawn reseeded, Mr. Jones comes to the realization that he will either have to give up his weekly game of golf or tell the family that there will be no vacation next summer.

You've all heard such stories about inept, incompetent, inefficient, and sometimes downright crooked contractors. There are internet web sites dedicated to contractor horror stories, television news magazine shows that highlight unscrupulous contractors, and organizations like the Better Business Bureau that monitor the activities of problem companies.

So in these circumstances, why in the world would anyone want to start his or her own contracting business? Fortunately, the vast majority of contractors are honest, hard-working folks who provide valuable services to the general public. They are talented men and women who have a positive vision of the future and a burning desire to use their talents for the betterment of not only themselves and their families but also for their community and fellow citizens.

Since founding a landscape design/build contracting company in 1976 with my wife, Kathy, I've learned much about starting and running a contracting business. Most of the learning was fun, but some of the most valuable lessons came from the school of hard knocks where we learned to profit both financially and personally from our mistakes. Our business grew with the help of many talented and dedicated associates and remains a success story to this day. We learned that building a successful business is a true team effort—whether the team consists of just a few people or many dozens.

This book covers many facets of the contracting business: It includes checklists for getting started, tips on marketing your services, and tips on how to price these services to make a reasonable profit. It presents ideas for hiring and managing employees and what to do when something goes wrong, either with those employees or with your customers. Along the way we'll include valuable tips, statistics, and facts about running your own business.

The goal is simple: we want you to know how to start your contracting business and keep it running smoothly, efficiently, and profitably.

The Contracting
Industry

The contracting industry is both huge and varied. All sorts of people and companies call themselves contractors. You have heard about Department of Defense contractors who build toilet seats for $600 and sell claw hammers for $450. We know of the hard-working and talented contractors who were instrumental in making the Apollo missions to the moon such a huge success. Some doctors are considered contractors because they sell their services to a particular hospital or clinic, and the same applies to some lawyers.

These are example of the far edges of the contracting industry: huge conglomerates with thousands of employees at one end of the spectrum and the individual specialist on the other end. On one hand, there are large corporations with millions or billions of dollars in assets, often owned by the public through stock offerings traded on a stock exchange, overseen by a large board of directors comprised of experts from many fields, and operated on a daily basis by dozens of highly paid executives and managers. At the other extreme, there is the one person who merely signs a contract with an individual or organization to perform a service. This person may have a partner and may have an executive assistant, but in general, these are very small entities and offer a very specific and limited service.

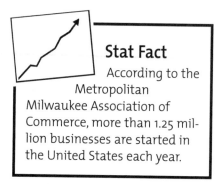

Stat Fact
According to the Metropolitan Milwaukee Association of Commerce, more than 1.25 million businesses are started in the United States each year.

If any of these examples apply to you, the reader, you need not read further. The intent of this book is to provide knowledge to either individual entrepreneurs or to small teams of entrepreneurs who want to start businesses providing contracting services to other businesses or individuals involved in property development. These contractors may provide services to individual home owners; developers of apartment, condominium, or commercial complexes; governments who develop public parks, plazas, and other recreational areas; or developers of residential subdivisions and housing developments.

In simple terms, there are two types of contractors who work with property development. First is the general contractor who organizes a project, hires other contractors to act as subcontractors, and is responsible for coordinating the activities of these subcontractors through the completion of the project. For example, the general contractor may be a home builder who engages the services of excavating contractors, carpenters, plumbers, electricians, and others to build a single home for a client. This

Beware!
Think of starting a new business as a marriage, full of commitment and desire. Like a marriage, you'll live with your business 24 hours a day, 365 days a year, through good times and bad.

operation is usually referred as a "turnkey" because the general contractor bundles the services of several subcontractors into a single contract with his or her client.

The second type of contractor is the independent contractor. These contractors work one-on-one with their clients and do not work under the direction of a general contractor. Many projects will have both types of contractors working in conjunction with each other. A client may hire a general contractor to build a new home, and also hire, under separate contracts, a landscape contractor to plan and install the outdoor spaces, a driveway installer to lay asphalt, and an irrigation company to install an automatic sprinkler system.

This book will focus on those contractors, both general and independent, who provide the services and material required to develop homes, office buildings, subdivisions, and similar projects. If you have the desire to become what I'll call a "property development" contractor, then this book is for you. I'll help you determine if you are the right type of person for such an undertaking. Then, I'll discuss the nitty-gritty of getting started. A lot of time will be spent on how to profitably price your product and service. Troubleshooting problem employees and clients will be another important topic. Finally, I'll tell you why it important to PANIC in order to be successful.

The Players

Developing a property can be a very complex and time-consuming undertaking. A wide range of experts are needed for a successful property development project. In general, there are two types of contractors involved with the development process: those who generally work on the inside of a building and those who work on the exterior of the building or in the landscape. Following is a list of contractors found working at property development projects. The list is not inclusive; there are additional contractors who have a special niche in the industry. Some contractors specialize in maintenance and repair, while others work with new construction; many do both.

Inside contractors include

- architects,
- engineers,
- interior designers,
- carpenters,
- plumbers,
- electricians,
- cabinetmakers,
- drywall contractors,
- flooring and tiling contractors,
- heating and air conditioning specialists,
- insulation contractors,

▲

- painters and paperhangers,
- security systems specialists, and
- masons.

Outside contractors include

- landscape architects,
- engineers,
- grading and excavating companies,
- asphalt companies,
- lighting experts,
- irrigation specialists,
- landscape contractors,
- surveyors,
- deck and patio builders,
- painters,
- swimming pool builders, and
- waterproofers.

Many times, for example a landscape architect will be responsible for the design of the exterior of the property, and an architect will design the building itself. Each may be responsible for ensuring that her designs are properly built. Each may hire other contractors to complete the work. These subcontractors may actually work for the architect/landscape architect and not for the owner of the property. They will schedule their work with the architect/landscape architect who, in turn, will coordinate the activities of all the subcontractors.

Another type of contractor is the design/build firm. This type of contracting company has trained architects and/or designers who provide plans for the development, assist the owners with obtaining the required permits for construction, and provide their own work force to complete the actual construction. In some cases, subcontractors may be used for services that the design/build company does not provide—usually very skilled services such as cabinetmaking or work that requires expensive equipment such as bulldozers and backhoes.

Of course, a property owner can act as his own general contractor. However, in order to be successful the owner must have the time to coordinate all the activities. Typically, he should be on-site daily to be sure that materials are delivered on time, that subcontractors are performing their work according to the plans, and often most important, authorized changes in the plans. (Imagine going on vacation for a week and returning to the project the following Monday morning and finding that your brand new kitchen was painted metallic gold rather than the soft yellow you thought you had selected.)

He must also understand the work of each of the subcontractors so that the work is coordinated in the proper sequence. There is nothing worse during the course of a project than having to undo work that has already been done. Imagine you are the general contractor and the driveway contractor has just completed his work: excavating and grading, installation of a 12-inch gravel base, and then laying three inches of asphalt. Then, the next day your plumber shows up with a huge backhoe and informs you that he must dig a trench 8-feet deep right through your new driveway so that he can install the septic system.

These are nightmare scenarios that have actually happened. Proper time management and knowledge of all facets of the work are vitally important to a successful project. Contractors of all types must know not only their own areas of expertise but also be able to communicate with and understand the basic work of the other contactors they work with.

Economic Importance

"Entrepreneurs and their small enterprises are responsible for almost all the economic growth in the United States."

—President Ronald Reagan

The contracting industry is vital to the economy of the United States. During good economic times, contractors are often the engine that keeps a local economy vibrant. Whenever you drive past a new subdivision, take a look at the number of different types of trucks and vans that enter the development each morning; note the different types of equipment being used by these workers. And think about the families that these workers are supporting. Their work helps support industries like department and appliance stores, grocery stores, and restaurants. During times of economic struggle, the most creative of these companies remain busy and viable with remodeling projects as well as providing maintenance and repair services. However when building and development slow down, the entire economy suffers as many employers lay off portions of their staff.

The contracting industry is not for the faint of heart. However, for those who have the resources, the talent, and the desire to become a contractor, the rewards can be substantial.

Stat Fact
According to industry sources, 90 percent of businesses in the U.S. construction industry employ fewer than 20 workers. Small construction businesses are a critical part of a vital economic sector and the U.S. economy as a whole.

Not only financial rewards but also quality of life issues are enhanced by owning your own successful contracting business.

So grab your hard hat, and jump right in to learn what it takes to become a successful and profitable contractor.

Chapter 1 Highlights

* The contracting industry is very large and diverse.

* Contractors are important and valuable contributors to local and regional economies.

* Profitable and rewarding opportunities abound for creative and talented entrepreneurs.

Bright Idea

If you are currently working for a contractor and plan to open your own business, don't assume that your customers will automatically move their business to your new company. Most customers are more loyal to a business than to an individual employee.

Why Become a
Contractor?

Becoming a contractor is a unique endeavor because contractors work out among their fellow citizens, unlike most retail or professional businesses who draw customers to their establishments. Contractors, on the other hand, spend most of their time away from their office or home base, working in or at their the homes, apartment buildings, offices, or on the property of others.

Contractors Are Important to their Communities

Contractors do much more than develop property. In many ways they improve the quality of life for their clients and their communities. For many clients, their homes are their castles, their property their domains. They spend countless hours in and around their homes and feel it is important to be comfortable with their surroundings. All have their own individual likes and dislikes. While one may require a quiet but colorful garden for introspective thought, another may need a hi-tech "great room" for entertaining friends and family. For many businesses, image is an important factor in their success. Perhaps a large fountain with multicolored lights is what they need, or a comfortable meeting room with the most modern communications equipment. Most municipalities have specific requirements and standards for the design of subdivisions, park land, and urban spaces. Creative contractors meet the varying needs of all these groups, completing their work in ways that will improve the health and welfare of the community.

Contractors also improve and ensure the safety of their clients. Proper design and construction of the spaces that people use for living, work, and recreation ensure a safe environment for these activities. Contractors are knowledgeable about local building codes as well as industry-accepted methods of installation. Following is a list of the areas where construction contractors improve the safety of the community and the people who live and work there:

- Provide *safe working conditions* for their employees
- Require employees to use *safety equipment* such as eye/ear protection and hard hats
- Ensure that buildings are *fire safe*
- Use methods of construction to ensure the *structural quality* of a building
- Design proper surface grading to provide *acceptable drainage* of rainwater
- Install handicap ramps and railings to *meet building codes*
- Install septic systems for *environmental safety*
- Design sight safety triangles at roadway and driveway intersection for *safe driving conditions*

Owning and managing your own business can be very rewarding—both mentally and financially. However, do not think that it is always a bed of roses. Remember that the rose gardens we see at homes and parks not only have beautiful flowers but are also full of sharp thorns. Operating your own business is much like the rose garden. The vibrant colors of the garden provide beauty and joy to passersby, but for those who get too close and do not pay attention to what they are doing, the sharp thorns can cause pain and discomfort. As you will learn later in the book, paying close attention to the details of your daily work will keep you from being stuck by the thorny issues that surround most businesses.

Do You Have What it Takes?—Part I

Contractors come in all sizes, shapes, and temperaments. But the one trait they all seem to have in common is a burning desire to start and operate their own business. If you have this burning desire to become your own boss, to work independently, to make all the important decisions required to run a successful business and you are willing to assume full responsibility for your decisions, you pass the first test on starting your own business. You also have to be willing to spend long hours and make many personal sacrifices to achieve success. There will be times when your family life will suffer because of the demands of your business. Do you have a good partner or spouse who understands and accepts these demands? Starting a business is difficult and stressful. It's vitally important to have a supportive family to get through the tough times. Finally, you need to have enough self-confidence to stand by your decisions as well as enough self-discipline to persevere and build your new business.

One of the intangible and hard-to-define qualities found in the most effective business owners is the ability to stand back and look at the big picture. Much like the race car drivers of the past, successful business owners must be able to understand and recognize the multitude of situations that affect the daily activities of their business. The race car driver, for obvious reasons, is concerned with speed. He will only win the race if he crosses the finish line first. However, pure speed is not the only factor in winning the race. While driving as fast as he can, the driver must be aware of tire pressure, engine temperature, and the front end of the car that controls steering, among many other things. These factors influence both the speed and the sustainability of the car. Low tire pressure will make the car more difficult to steer, which will affect speed; high engine temperature will effect engine performance and also reduce speed. The driver must be able to look at the big picture and understand how the smallest of details interact and influence the final result of the race. The best drivers are also able to look at an anomaly and realize that it may not affect the performance of their car. Today, drivers, much like modern business owners, are assisted by computer technology and a team that helps to interpret the data. But this help does not reduce the importance of understanding how the numerous bits and pieces of a business react and influence each other—and as important, when to ignore what seems to be a problem when it is of little or no significance to the operation of the business.

Do You Have the Proper Background?

Individual skills are extremely important to succeeding in the contracting industry. Some are natural, and many can be learned. The ability to use and improve both natural and learned skills is an important factor in developing a successful business. Some jobs require more natural ability than others; other jobs rely largely on learned skills. However, it is important to develop your skills to the highest possible level.

Those of you who have a desire to enter the design field, such as architecture or landscape architecture, must have artistic and creative instincts. The ability to think abstractly and visualize outcomes is extremely important. Creative solutions to development challenges separate the outstanding firm from the average one. Most industry associations have annual awards competitions where companies or individuals have the opportunity to present their best projects, their best ideas, to their peers. The most creative of these projects stand out and set the standards of excellence for their respective industries.

However, natural skill and ability is not enough. Consider professional golf. It is universally agreed that Tiger Woods is the most talented pro currently on the PGA tour. He may be the best of all time. But he did not get to the top merely by using the talents he was born with. His father worked tirelessly with young Tiger to hone his skills; he perfected his swing and trained his mind to withstand the rigors of intense competition. Even after winning many major golf tournaments, Tiger keeps working with his coaches to improve his swing so that he can continue to stay ahead of the competition. Other great golfers, who will remain nameless out of respect for their past achievements, suddenly lost their ability to win. Some dropped out of the PGA tour; others failed to meet the high standards and lost the right to compete. While many of these golfers had the natural ability to play excellent golf, they, for often unexplainable reasons, failed to maintain their play at a high level. Like entrepreneurs who start their own businesses, professional golfers must enhance their natural skills with learned skills.

There are a couple of different methods of obtaining learned skills—formal education and on-the-job training. We will explore each further.

Tip...

Smart Tip
The internet is a great source of information. To find accredited colleges in architecture, landscape architecture, and engineering go to www.naab.org, www.alsa.org, and www.abet.org.

Formal Education

Architects, landscape architects, engineers, and others in the professional field typically earn undergraduate or graduate degrees in their field. Four to five years of college are required for an undergraduate degree; to obtain a Master's degree, another one to three years of study is usually required. Many colleges will allow students to earn a Master's degree even if their undergraduate degree is in a field unrelated to architecture, landscape architecture, or engineering.

There are excellent opportunities for those who do not wish, or are unable, to attend a full four-year college program. Technical schools, usually offering two-year degree programs, are a great place to learn a new trade or to improve on a skill you presently have. These programs do not require the rigorous high school cur-

Smart Tip *Tip...*

The web site www.collegeboard.com has an extensive search engine for finding colleges of all types throughout the United States.

riculum and pre-admission testing needed to be accepted at four-year colleges. Technical schools offer degrees in the construction trades such as plumbing, carpentry, and landscaping. They also offer programs in business management, marketing, and real estate for those who intend on someday starting their own business in the property development industry. Currently nearly 2,000 technical schools in the United States offer associate degree programs in the construction trades and horticulture/landscaping.

On-the-Job Training (OJT)

Those of you who have been in the military likely understand the term "OJT." After surviving eight weeks of torturous Basic Training, you were given an MOS (military occupational specialty) and assigned to a post. If, for example, the Army decided that it needed a clerk-typist, you might be assigned to a company headquarters office to learn typing and filing. No experience needed; just show up for work and your superior would show you what to do. Over the following weeks and months, you'd learn your job while doing it. Little, if any, formal education was provided. If you learned the job quickly, you'd be promoted from private to specialist, and hopefully to sergeant. Each promotion would bring more responsibility and higher wages.

In the construction business, OJT is a common way for employees to learn the trade. New inexperienced employees are assigned to a work crew led by an experienced foreman or crew leader. It's the job of the foreman to complete each job or project according to the specifications established for the project and to finish it at or under budget. Her job is also to train new employees how to do their particular tasks.

As in the military example new employees are given simple tasks at first and then move on to more complex and skilled work as they master each task.

An important part of OJT is making mistakes! All employees will make mistakes at some time during their career, and new employees typically make more mistakes than more experienced ones. The key to mistakes is the ability to learn from them. Unfortunately, some employees make the same mistake over and over, usually resulting in a short term of employment. However, those who do learn from mistakes and errors eventually become much better and productive employees. And, most important for those who intend on starting their own contracting business, understanding and learning from your past mistakes will make you a better teacher of new employees; the result will be that your business is more productive, successful, and profitable.

Beware!

Driving records can be good indicators of learning from past mistakes. Drivers who repeat the same violation over and over do not learn from their mistakes. Be very cautious when hiring employees with poor driving records.

Lloyd Price

Your first reaction is probably "Who"? Well, back in the early days of rock n' roll music, before the Beatles became famous, an up-and-coming singer from New Orleans named Lloyd Price released a hit record called "(You've Got) Personality" in which the singer croons:

> *But over and over*
> *I'll be a fool for you*
> *'cause you got personality*

Now don't get in a tizzy and think that we are suggesting potential clients are foolish or that business owners who have a strong personality will instantly become successful. However, personality traits are important when considering starting up your own contracting business. Successful business owners in any field have some characteristics in common. Among the most important are the following.

Discipline and Determination

Think again of Tiger Woods and other great golfers. They all combine their natural athletic ability with discipline and determination. They are disciplined in the way they practice and in the way they approach each shot. Week in and week out they practice and set up each shot in precisely the same way. They are also determined enough to keep their minds on the game and their goal (of winning) always in sight. They have incredible ability to focus on the task at hand; the last shot they made, good or bad, is a distant memory and has absolutely no affect on their next shot. They also persevere through good times and bad. Consider Phil Mickelson who won the Masters golf tournament after laboring on the PGA tour for 12 years. Only three previous winners of this prestigious tournament, which started in 1934, won it at a later point in their career.

Self-Reliance

Self-confidence is critical. Business ownership is often a lonely life. President Harry Truman had a sign on his desk which read, "The Buck Stops Here," indicating that he was responsible for decision making. He could not pass crucial decisions on to someone else. Similarly, in order to start up and run a successful contracting business, the owner must be willing to make these decisions, often alone. While she can rely on her staff to provide data and information, the buck stops with the owner. Oftentimes some sort of risk is involved. Owners face numerous financial decisions, many of them with inherent risk, such as future changes in interest rates, consumer confidence, and spending habits. Unexpected changes in any of these can lead to difficult financial times for any business. Other risks might include predicting the mood and tastes of consumers. A contractor may decide to roll out a new advertising campaign targeted at a particular segment of the community or promoting a particular product. If consumers reject the service or product, the company will suffer.

Good Health

Operating a contracting business is both physically and mentally stressful. Early mornings, followed by long days, and six-day weeks are very common throughout the contracting industry. Contractors must be in excellent health, both physically and mentally, in order to achieve success.

Excellent Time Management

A well-organized manager earns the respect not only of fellow employees, but also of clients. Everyday an owner is bombarded with requests, often these are really demands, on his or her time. Foremen ask for direction about a current project; an assistant requests clarification of information needed to complete a job estimate; a client calls asking why some service was not done properly; a supplier calls to reschedule a delivery; and a magazine salesperson calls needing information for the current advertisement, which has a deadline of today. All this, and the owner has an important meeting with a prospective client in one hour. Oh yes, and don't forget to sign today's payroll checks. Most contracting businesses are like a busy beehive, especially in the morning. An owner must be able to prioritize his tasks, adjust the daily schedule to solve true emergencies, and keep the operation moving forward as smoothly as possible. Of particular importance in time management is organizing the work crews on a daily basis so that time is not wasted and clients kept waiting. Efficient foremen know exactly where they are going, what type of work they will do, and what tools they need to complete the job. If an owner is too busy with other tasks, money is lost while employees are getting paid to sit and wait for instructions.

Time management is not only important on a daily basis but also on a long-term basis. As the backlog of work increases, owners must be able to accurately project how long each project will take so that they can accurately schedule future projects. One of the worst things a contracting company can do is promise a client "we'll be there next week" and then, for no reason apparent to the client, show up in three weeks. A company may use a chart like the one in the Sample Work Schedule below.

In the Sample Work Schedule, if another client, Mr. Allen, prefers to work with Charlie, the owner knows that he cannot promise to start the Allen project until early June. Similarly, if Jane is extremely talented in a particular task, the owner knows he cannot send her out to complete this type of work until late May.

Time management encompasses much more that merely organizing a daily calendar. It is crucial to the success of a contracting business.

Sample Work Schedule

Foreman	May 1	May 8	May 15	May 22
Charlie	Jones	Jones O'Brien	Smith	Mueller
Jane	Wilson Hellman	Carson	Carson	(open)
Andy	Murphy	McCarthy	(open)	(open)

Do You Have What it Takes?—Part II

Beyond personality issues are a host of factors that contractor owners must have in order to succeed. The best and most successful contractors have a good balance of technical skills and business management expertise. As you learned earlier, many contractors are blessed with the natural skills to do their jobs. Most are craftsmen and women who pay careful attention to detail, avoid sloppy work, and finish their work with confidence and pride. They are able to step back from a completed project and say to themselves and their co-workers, "Job well done!" They are confident that their clients will say the same thing.

Continuing Education

As skilled as they may be, many contractors like to keep up to date with the latest advances in their field by taking advantage of opportunities for continuing education. There are many avenues available for learning about new products and techniques:

- Seminars presented by suppliers of the materials a contractor purchases.
- How-to seminars given by home improvement stores like Home Depot and Lowe's.
- Conferences and classes offered or sponsored by industry associations.
- Technical colleges; for example in the northern climes, landscaping classes are offered during the winter months when most landscape companies have more time to spend on formal education.
- Industry-specific magazines and newspapers.
- The government sponsored Small Business Administration (www.sba.gov) offers help to all small businesses.

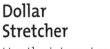

Dollar Stretcher
Use the internet and do a Google search for "contractor magazines," and find opportunities to receive free magazine subscriptions that focus on your specialty.

Tools

Contractors don't like to admit it, but many members of the public, their potential clients, are able to do similar work. Perhaps not quite as well and certainly not as fast, but they can do many tasks that contractors are experts at. The DIY (Do-It-Yourself) retail market is huge; the combined revenues of Home Depot and Lowe's are over $125 billion; several cable television stations specialize in home improvement and remodeling.

However, beyond their natural skills and personalities, contractors possess two things that most of the public does not have. First, they have the time to do the work. Most homeowners and amateurs can only work nights and weekends; their regular jobs prevent them from working full time on their projects. Most homeowners do not want to live in their homes for extended periods without running water or with a hole in the roof, or go through the entire winter without a driveway. Contractors have the ability to complete a project quickly and with minimal disruption to their client's household.

Second, contractors have the right tools to do the job. While the equipment rental business is fairly large, many homeowners are uncomfortable using expensive tools. Some tools and equipment are not available for rent due to liability issues; other equipment, such as a dump truck usually is not available on a short-term basis. Often, when a homeowner rents a particular tool, he botches the job because he does not have enough experience to do a proper job.

Having the right tools is one of the keys to success in the contracting industry. A landscape contractor reported to us that when he first started he used a hand-held sod remover when preparing plant beds; on one of his first jobs, he and a worker spent the better part of two days removing sod by hand. The result was not only sore arms and tendonitis in his wrists, but a lower profit due to the time it took to do the task. The next week he purchased a gas-powered sod cutter for several thousand dollars, a very large expense for the young company. But the time savings he achieved by using newer and better technology allowed him to pay for the sod cutter in a single season. Instead of spending two days removing sod, he was able to complete the same work in a few hours, often with less manpower as well. In fact, his sales and profits actually increased because he was able to move on to the next job much more quickly.

Learn the Lingo

Contactors often work together to finish projects. Their working relationship may not be formal as they might merely be working on a project at the same time. However, many contractor jobs overlap. Contractors have to understand what the others are doing so that they do not "step on each other's toes." All of them should be able to read and understand blueprints of the building and the landscaping so that the materials they are installing do not interfere or conflict with what the other contractor is doing. For example, the irrigation contractor must be able to read the landscape plan and the grading plan in order to efficiently design the sprinkler system; the low-voltage outdoor lighting specialist must understand the electrical plans in order to design a lighting plan that reduces voltage drop and does not conflict with the full-voltage lights specified for the home.

A development project comes together more successfully when all the participants understand each other's responsibilities and what the scope of their work includes. While they do not necessarily need to know how to do the work of the other contractors, they must understand the concepts and terminology used by them.

Money Issues

President Thomas Jefferson once wrote "never spend your money before you have it." This little truism has wide implications for the contracting industry because of the seasonal and cyclical nature of the business. In Chapter 6 I discuss how to establish a budget and the importance of cash flow. But first there are two important issues relating to money that everyone contemplating starting up his or her own business should understand.

A Nest Egg

Conventional wisdom states that a new business owner should have savings in the bank to cover at least six months of personal expenses. Every potential business owner must take the time to learn how much money he or she has spent over the past 12 months and estimate total expenses for the next six months. The attitude should be "since I will be working without a guaranteed income stream, how will I survive for at least the next six months?" Use your checkbook, bank statement, or credit/debit card statements to compile a list of all your projected expenses—mortgage, taxes, utilities, insurance, food, and recreation. If your spouse has a secure job, his or her take-home pay can be used to reduce the amount of savings you need. If you do not have the ready cash to survive at least six months, you would be wise to postpone starting up your business until you have the necessary funds.

Your savings should be invested in a conservative, high yielding money market account that offers free checking and has few, if any, fees. One source for information is on the internet at www.bankrate.com. Many financial magazines also include up-to-date interest rate information on a weekly basis.

Start-Up Funds

Beyond providing a nest egg for personal living, any new business also needs enough capital to survive four to six months of business. Because it usually takes some time for a new enterprise to attract enough business to ensure a secure cash flow, having enough ready cash is critical. Operating expenses for things such as salaries, wages, rent, utilities, supplies, advertising, and perhaps bank and interest payments. Sources of these funds usually are loans from banks or individuals, accumulated personal savings, and even credit cards.

A Good Credit Rating

The financial demands on a new contracting company can be enormous. Not only do employees expect to receive their wages every week or two, suppliers expect to be paid every month, possibly even within ten days. Clients, on the other hand, often do not see an urgency to pay immediately upon completion of the work. Some clients seem to think that contractors are banks and that they can pay off their invoice over several months. The situation can be helped by requesting a down payment from a client before work begins. However, a key ingredient to success is earning a good credit rating so that your suppliers will send you a bill once a month for the items you purchased. A good credit rating will also allow you to purchase vehicles and equipment and borrow the funds from your bank.

The Catch-22 of buying materials on credit is the ability to pay in a timely manner without incurring late and/or finance charges. Chapter 6 delves into the subject of managing your cash flow in much more detail. Remember, a good credit rating will allow you to establish charge accounts at your suppliers, but only by paying the suppliers according to their requirements will you maintain your good credit rating.

There are three companies in the United States that maintain credit information on individuals: Equifax, Experian, and TransUnion LLC. Contact information on these companies may be found in the Appendix. It is a good idea to check your credit rating from time to time to ensure that there are no errors in the report.

> ## Smart Tip
> *Tip...*
>
> Get to know your banker! It is not enough just to swing by the bank and make deposits; you should get to know a personal banker at the branch where you do your banking. Over time, she will understand your business and your financial needs. She'll be in a good position to advise you about interest rates, borrowing, and how to best manage your cash.

Management Expertise

An important piece of the puzzle needed to answer the question "Do you have what it takes?" is the ability to manage the enterprise. You have seen that contractors must be able to manage their own time, be disciplined, and be self-reliant. However, they must also be able to manage the activities and turmoil that usually surround them on a daily basis. A workplace is a dynamic community of people with varying backgrounds. While it is true that a company is much like a family, it is also an individual business. Often business decisions conflict with personal feelings; good managers must be able to separate emotion from hard reality.

Managing People

Managing people is a true art. Each person has a unique personality that sometimes conflicts with another person's. However, because both work for the same organization, they must be able to work together for a common goal. Personal habits, hygiene, political viewpoints, and family life are often sources of personal conflict. A contractor-owner has to learn how to balance the effects of individual personalities for the common good.

You have heard about the sports team whose talent is not highly regarded; however, its coach has the ability to push each player and enable each to perform at a level above their natural talents. He's able to generate positive chemistry on the team, with the result that the individual team members play their best and the team wins the championship. For a more specific example, let's assume that Joe is a long-term employee who has much in common with the boss: both attended college in the same city, love to play golf, and have sons enrolled in the same school; they often see each other at functions unrelated to their jobs. However, for personal family reasons, Joe's production, attitude, and attendance have become a problem. The boss has several discussions with Joe who becomes more defensive and angry with each meeting. Joe's behavior finally begins to negatively affect several of the office staff. The result is that company sales decline, the atmosphere in the office is dark and dismal, productivity suffers, and clients become upset with their service. Ultimately the boss will have to make the difficult decision of whether to fire Joe. He will have to put personal feelings aside, take a look at the big picture, and make the ultimate decision about Joe's fate.

Communication Management

Almost everyone fears public speaking. When preparing to speak before a group, most people get extremely nervous, their palms sweat, their stomach churns, and their voice cracks. With practice, most people learn that if they really know their topic, their nervousness disappears once they begin to talk. Luckily for business owners, public speaking is not a daily or even weekly event.

Still, successful owners must have excellent communication skills. Time, money, and reputation can be lost by owners who do not

Bright Idea

Toastmasters International offers programs through which members learn public speaking by speaking to groups and working with other members in a supportive environment. Information can be found at www.toastmasters.org.

communicate clearly with both employees and clients. Many clients have preconceived ideas about what a contractor plans to do; oftentimes they do not read contracts and proposals carefully enough to really understand what they are getting. Usually, they do not understand blueprints; sometimes, they have a vision from a photograph in a home improvement magazine. It's critical that a contractor-owner has the ability to clearly explain the services he offers and exactly what he proposes to do for the client. In the case of landscaping, it's important that the client understand that it takes time for a landscape to mature; unlike a new kitchen or bathroom, the final product in not realized immediately upon completion of the work.

Owners must also be able to accurately communicate with employees. Because projects are often changed and adjusted in mid-stream, good communication between the owner and the foreman is needed for the project to proceed accurately and on time. In addition, two-dimensional drawings are sometimes difficult to translate into the three-dimensional world. The contractor must not only communicate what must be done with accurate and legible drawings but also must be able to explain verbally what the drawings mean.

Organization Management

How many times have you heard someone say, "the left hand doesn't know what the right hand is doing." As business owners, you would much rather hear, "it went off like clockwork." Contractors are often away from the office much of the day, and unless they have a very small family business, they do not really know what happens at the office. Employees are very aware of a disorganized boss who is out-of-touch with the day-to-day operations of the office and runs from one task to another in a seemingly haphazard way. Most owners are not aware of the office gossip and whispers that make the rounds; they probably would be appalled at what they would hear. Unfortunately, an owner's own chaotic style often filters down to the office staff. However, if an owner implements a good organizational chart, with the assistance of employees who perform the work, each employee will know his own responsibilities and, as important, the responsibilities of every other employee. In this way the company will operate more efficiently, profitably, and mistake-free. Chapter 9 goes into more detail about organizational charts.

Send in the Delegation

A key to organizational success is the ability of an entrepreneur to delegate responsibilities to other employees. Very few business owners have the ability to perform all the tasks required to operate their business. They are likely to be experts at some things, very good at others, and nearly hopeless at others. Because most entrepreneurs have loads of confidence in their abilities, it is hard for many to admit to themselves, "I'm not very good in this area, I need help, and this is how I intend to achieve it."

Delegating authority to others can be a difficult task not only because it may be difficult to find the right person to handle the tasks, but also because it is hard for an entrepreneur to give up some of the control of his business. The process of delegating involves four steps:

1. Finding good people who are trustworthy and have the expertise to be successful in the area concerned.

2. Hiring the person and incorporating him into your company.

3. Giving him the ball.

4. Allowing him to run with it.

The best entrepreneurs routinely monitor the activities of these employees but do not constantly look over their shoulders, micromanage their activities, or reverse their decisions without very good cause.

While the ability to delegate is important, overdelegating can become a problem. The owner may become too far removed from the daily activities of the business. The art of delegating is also the art of team building; owners must understand how all the pieces of the business fit together to form the whole. The risk in overdelegating is that decision making becomes too decentralized, communication breaks down, and the business becomes inefficient.

Chapter 2 Highlights

* Contractors enhance the safety of individuals as well as the community at large.

* Contractor-owners have the burning desire to operate their own business and have the knowledge and experience, either through formal education or on-the-job training, to be successful.

* As business owners, contractors must be disciplined and determined, self reliant, in good health, and practice excellent time management.

* Contractors have the advantage over the general public because they keep up with the latest advances in their particular field, have the best tools to do the job, and understand the common terminology used in the various disciplines of the property development industry.

* Contractors can be successful if their finances are in good order, they have the ability to manage people and communicate with employees and clients, and they know how to organize their employees for maximum efficiency.

* The ability to delegate responsibilities is critical to success.

3

The Business
Plan

A business plan is a written document
that summarizes how a business owner intends to organize her
business and how it will organize itself so that the business will
succeed. It defines the strategy that will be used to establish,
operate, and market the venture. The business plan has value
because it forces the entrepreneur to engage in the planning

process through which she will gain a better understanding of the industry, the business, and the various options available. The business plan is also a valuable selling tool that can be used when obtaining loans from banks or individual investors.

Business plans come in many forms. Many are very detailed documents while others are more informal checklists. A typical outline of a business plan follows:

Executive Summary

Broad overview of the company, management, and goals

Description

Your business

Geographical location

Industry history and future

Features and Advantages of Your Products or Services

Description

Competitive advantage

Future potential

Marketing

Market size and trends

Competition

Strategy for competing

Potential customer base

Estimating Sales

Marketing plan and strategy

Sales plan

Pricing

Advertising

Production

Equipment costs

Inventory requirements

Physical plant requirements

Geographic location

Availability of materials and supplies

Human Resources

Labor force availability; hiring

Skills required

Stat Fact
Business plans can take several months to prepare. Approximately 90 percent of entrepreneurs use outside professional advisors such as accountants or lawyers; nearly 70 percent attend business plan seminars.

Compensation

Benefits

Training

Management

Key personnel

Compensation

Strengths and weaknesses

Organization and ownership

Board of directors

Outside advisors (accountant, lawyer)

Finance

Source of funds

Break-even analysis

Existing liabilities

Projected sales and expenses

Internal financial controls

Risk Planning, strategies for:

Unfavorable industrywide growth trends

Low sales

Lack of skilled labor

Price cutting by competition

Costs exceeding budget

Recession

Schedule

Timing of activities before opening

Timing of activities after opening

Mission Statement

Every business has a purpose for its existence. A written mission statement, usually one
to four sentences long, says what your company
is, what you do, what you stand for, and why it's
important. An example of a poorly written mission statement is: "We build fine homes." A

Dollar Stretcher

There are many sources of information about how to pre-pare a business plan. One excellent source is the Small Business Administration (www.sba.gov), which provides assistance over the internet. Numerous books covering business plans can be found on the internet at Amazon (www.amazon.com), Barnes and Noble (www.bandn.com), and other online book sellers.

much better example is: "We are dedicated to providing services and solutions that meet the dreams of our clients. Quality construction is delivered with friendliness, professionalism, individual pride, and company spirit." The best mission statements focus on satisfying customer needs rather than on the products that are sold. Certainly everyone wants to have a fine home, but it is more important for a client to know how they will get that fine home. The mission statement can be used to communicate important information to both clients and employees. The client will have positive feelings about hiring a company with a compelling and personal mission statement, and employees will understand the goals and objectives of the company they work for.

Financing Your Business

There are two ways to finance your new business: equity and debt. Equity financing involves raising money (capital) by issuing common stock to investors. These investors will have an ownership stake in the new business. Often, this type of financing comes directly from the owners themselves; they invest their personal savings in the business. Other sources of funds may come from friends or relatives who have an interest in helping the new enterprise. Caution must be used when taking money from friends and relatives; personal relationships may be ruined if the business fails and these friends lose their investment. Business owners who raise capital in this manner must explain their business plan carefully and make it clear to potential investors that there are risks associated with their investment.

Venture capitalists are another source of equity financing. These are wealthy individuals or companies who look for start-ups in which to invest their money. Generally, however, venture capitalists prefer to invest in companies whose stock is publicly traded on a stock exchange so they can sell their shares for a profit when the company is successful. Therefore, small contracting businesses are usually not appealing to these investors.

Debt financing is achieved by borrowing money from a bank, credit union, or the U.S. Small Business Administration. These entities rely heavily on the business plan, financial forecasts, and the personal finances of the owners of the business. A new business is much more likely to obtain debt financing if the owners have committed a significant portion of the capital required for the business to get off the ground.

The "OOPS" Factor

Heraclitus, one of the most significant of all the ancient Greek philosophers, lived about 2,500 years ago, before the more well-known Socrates and Plato. His idea that the universe is constantly changing and that there is an underlying reason for this change still holds true in modern Western thinking. In one of his writings, he penned "The unapparent connection is more powerful than the apparent one." This is like our modern law of unintended consequences: all actions have at least one unintended consequence; and each cause has more than one effect, including unforeseen effects. These unforeseen effects may be positive, negative, or potentially a problem. When entrepreneurs make business decisions and set company policies, they must be aware of unintended consequences and take every reasonable measure to prevent or eliminate negative surprises.

It is easy to find examples of unintended consequences. In 1996, vice presidential candidate Jack Kemp said, "Every time this century we've lowered the tax rates across the board on employment, on saving, investment and risk-taking in this economy, revenues went up, not down." One might think that lower taxes would reduce the revenues of the federal government; the seemingly unintended consequence is that the opposite is true. Kemp is a well known conservative, but Presidents Franklin Delano Roosevelt and John F. Kennedy, both Democrats, also believed that high tax rates are a hindrance to the economy.

Consider the small contracting business that had a policy requiring its employees to look neat and clean while on the job; to this end the company decided to give employees new uniforms whenever theirs became permanently soiled or worn. The employees loved this policy but began wearing their uniforms for all sorts of activities, from participating in a weekend rugby match to crawling under their automobile to change the oil. Soon, employees were requesting replacement uniforms every week or two. While the intended consequence of the policy was met, its employees looked great on the job, the unintended consequence was that expenses for uniforms skyrocketed far beyond what the company expected. It did not take the company long to place strict limits on the number of free uniforms they would issue.

Savvy entrepreneurs look at decisions and policies from all angles, attempting to avoid unintended consequences.

Chapter 3 Highlights

* The well-developed business plan has been called a blueprint for success. It is a valuable tool that can be used to obtain financing, to communicate your goals and objective to employees, and to hold them responsible for results. It can also be used to track your progress over time and make mid-course corrections if needed.

* Financing the business can be achieved through a combination of equity and debt.

* Be aware of The Law of Unintended Consequences when making policy decisions.

4

Law and the
G-Man

Title 26 of the Federal Code, also referred to as
the Internal Revenue Code, is made up of 20 volumes and is
nearly 17,000 pages long. It includes laws covering income
taxes, payroll taxes, gift taxes, estate taxes, and excise taxes.
Most states have their own tax regulations covering similar
taxes and tack on rules and regulations covering items like

workers' compensation insurance and sales taxes. In addition, agencies such as the Social Security Administration and the Equal Employment Opportunity Commission issue their own pamphlets regulating employers. Employer compliance with the myriad of rules and regulations is a daunting task, but one that cannot be ignored. A properly established and organized business can cope with the government bureaucracy fairly easily if it understands the basic rules and establishes internal procedures for following those rules.

Business Structure

The first task in setting up your own contracting business is to decide exactly what form, in legal terms, you want your business to be. This legal structure largely determines how much risk the owner takes on and how the government will treat his income. An entrepreneur should consult with his lawyer and accountant when deciding which form of business to use, and when consulting with these professionals, be sure to disclose all of your family assets and income, because these factors may influence their recommendations. The choices that business owners have when forming a new company are:

1. *Sole proprietor*. This form of business has no separate structure from its owner. Even though the sole proprietor may register a trade name like "Jane's Drywall Service," all assets, debts, tax liabilities, and risks belong to Jane. Sole proprietorship has several disadvantages. It may be harder to obtain financing, and the owner will have unlimited liability in the event the business is sued. This is the simplest form of business and is reserved for the individual entrepreneur.

2. *Partnership*. Formed when two or more individuals enter an agreement to manage a business, a partnership does not protect the individual liability of the owners. The partners manage the business and are equally and personally liable for debts and obligations of the business. Extreme care must be taken when forming a partnership because each partner is legally and financially responsible for the actions of the other partners. Like an S corporation (see below), the partnership does not pay taxes because the profits and losses are passed on directly to the partners.

3. *Limited liability company (LLC)*. Increasingly popular, the newest kid on the block is a hybrid structure that combines the limited liability of a corporation (S or C) with the tax advantages and flexibility of a partnership. The company is owned by members, as opposed to stockholders, and profits and losses are passed on directly to them. In some cases, a member may contribute services rather than money and, in turn, receive an interest in profits and losses.

4. *S corporation.* Usually reserved for smaller companies with fewer than 100 shareholders, an S corporation provides limited personal liability to its shareholders (owners) so that if the corporation is sued, the personal assets of the shareholders are protected from the lawsuit. The other significant issue with S corporations is that the corporation itself does not pay income taxes. All profits and losses are passed through to the individual shareholders according to the share of the stock each owns. Shareholders are liable for taxes even if they did not receive cash income from the company. The company itself is managed by a board of directors that appoints officers to take responsibility for day-to-day operations.

5. *C corporation.* Most large companies in the United States are C corporations. Like an S corporation, shareholders are protected from lawsuits and the company is managed by a board of directors. However, the corporation itself is taxed on its profits, and the shareholders are taxed on any dividends they receive. Shareholders must be aware that dividends are paid on after-tax profits, which results in double taxation because the shareholders are also personally liable for taxes on the dividends they receive.

When deciding on a business structure that meets both your business and personal needs, the entrepreneur should consider the following:

- *How vulnerable is your business to law suits?* Court dockets are full of suits against contractors. Is your specialty among those involved in numerous law suits by unhappy clients? If it is, then a corporation or LLC is the best for you.

- *Do you need to pull cash or capital out of the business?* Once you set up a corporation, you cannot generally take money out of it (even if it is your own money) without paying income taxes on the distribution.

- *Tax implications are another factor and should be discussed with your accountant.* For example, if you use a company vehicle for personal use, you may have to report the value of the personal use as additional income, and pay additional taxes.

- *The level of control you want to have over business operations should be discussed with your lawyer.* Corporations are managed by a board of directors and must make financial reports to stockholders. For very small companies, these boards may be comprised of only family members.

 Beware!
We know of a group of young men who decided to open a business together. One of them had the funds to finance the endeavor; others were proficient in sales and operations. Unfortunately, the sales and operations men treated the cash in the bank as their own money and used it for personal travel and entertainment expenses. Ultimately, the business failed, and the financier was left without any of his original investment.

But as the business grows, nonfamily members often join the Board and outsiders may invest in the company. It is also not unusual for several friends to join forces to open a new business. In this case, each individual may have different needs, lifestyles, and personal assets. The working relationship and order of authority should be determined during the very early phases of establishing a business.

- *The size and nature of the business also influences the structure.* Small companies that focus on limited services may be better run as sole proprietors or LLCs. Among these might be excavating contractors or roofing companies. However, large companies that require large amounts of capital, may have union employees, work on numerous projects at one time, and hire subcontractors usually benefit from a corporate structure.

Accounting Methods

There are two types of accounting methods that are used by small business: cash accounting and accrual accounting. The IRS has placed some restrictions on the use of the cash method, so the new contractor is advised to consult with his accountant to decide which is best for his business. While most accounting software programs use the accrual method, it is usually a simple matter for a good accountant to make the year-end adjustments needed to prepare an accurate tax return based on a cash accounting system.

The difference between the two methods is basically one of timing. When using the cash method, revenue is recognized and recorded on the company books when the money is actually received, and expenses are recognized when payment is made. However, when using the accrual method, revenues and expenses are recorded when incurred. Consider the following information:

K&K Contractors—Cash Accounting vs. Accrual Accounting

- December 7, 2006: Materials are purchased on credit by K&K for Smith project: $2,500
- December 10, 2006: Smith project is completed
- December 12, 2006: Smith is sent an invoice for $5,000
- December 31, 2006: Tax year ends for K&K Contractors
- January 7, 2007: Smith pays $5,000 to K&K
- January 30, 2007: $2,500 is paid by K&K to the supplier for Smith materials

The effect on the income statement of K&K Contractors varies by the accounting system used:

1. *Cash accounting.* Neither the $2,500 expense nor the $5,000 income is included in the 2006 income statement because the actual payment and receipt took place in 2007.

2. *Accrual accounting.* Both the $2,500 expense and the $5,000 income are included in the 2006 income statement even though the cash was not received until January 7 and the expense not paid until January 30.

As you can see, the accounting method used can have an effect on your taxes, both positive and negative. Both methods, however, offer legal strategies for accelerating expenses so that they occur in the current year and for deferring income into the following year. Obviously, care must be taken, and consultation and advice from your accountant is paramount.

Bankers, Lawyers, Accountants, and Insurance Agents

These specialists are crucial to a new business. However, although they may be experts in their own field, they may not really understand how your business operates. Even if they own and operate their own business, it is unlikely that they understand project management, inventory control, equipment needs, and the lingo of your trade. In order to profitably use their intelligence and expertise, the new business entrepreneur must work closely with these professionals; it is usually a mistake to turn a task over to one of them and think "It's OK, the accountant is handling it." In particular, tax and labor laws are extremely confusing and are subject to a certain amount of interpretation. The business owner must help the lawyer and accountant interpret the myriad of rules and regulations as they pertain to her specific contracting business.

A good relationship with a banker can both save money and enable to company to operate more smoothly. When looking for a bank to do business with, take along your business plan so that the bank can better understand your goals and objectives and how you will reach them. When a personal business banker understands the financial status of the business and the owners, he is in a good position to advise the company in a number of areas. Because most businesses borrow money from banks to purchase tools and equipment, the banker is a valuable resource for understanding interest rate trends and projections. Again, presenting a clear business plan assists in obtaining loans with the most favorable terms. The banker can also help establish a line of credit for companies that periodically need cash to support daily operations.

The final outside professional that contractors must have on their team is the insurance agent. Insurance has become a highly complex and specialized business covering all aspects of American life. Three areas of insurance are of particular interest to contractors: (1) general business and vehicles, (2) workers' compensation, and (3) health insurance. Rather than working with a single insurance company, it is often advantageous to work with an insurance agent who represents a number of different insurance companies. The agent can compare prices to ensure that the contractor is getting the best coverage at the best cost. Often, contracting companies will work with one agent to handle business, vehicle, and worker's compensation and another agent for health insurance. In this age of specialization, other agents may be engaged to find life insurance or long-term health insurance coverage if these are benefits that a business owners wishes to offer his employees.

Coping with the Government

Former President Ronald Reagan said during his presidency:

> *Government's view of the economy could be summed up in a few short phrases: If it moves, tax it. If it keeps moving, regulate it. And if it stops moving, subsidize it.*

> ## ⚠ Beware!
> Most contractors have inland marine insurance, which covers equipment other than vehicles. Premiums for this insurance may be based on either replacement cost, which will pay for new equipment to replace destroyed or stolen equipment, or on actual value, which is based on the current depreciated value of the equipment. Actual value insurance has much lower premiums than replacement cost insurance; however, the ultimate cost of replacing equipment is higher. Actual value insurance is usually recommended unless a contracting company generally works in unsafe neighborhoods.

No matter your politics, all business owners must deal with government rules and regulations. Most contractors don't like it, but have little choice except to cope as best they can. Certainly lawyers, accountants, bankers, and insurance agents can assist in the process, but the responsibility of complying with the numerous agency rules falls squarely on the shoulders of the business owner. Even though following government guidelines can be difficult, especially when rules and regulations are constantly changing, it is important for the contractor-owner to realize that ignorance of laws is never an excuse for noncompliance. In this section, I review the most common obligations businesses have in regard to the demands of their government. Fortunately, most of the information can be found on the internet at www.irs.gov. The accounts and/or forms that most new businesses must use to operate legally are:

- *Federal government*
  - Employer Identification Number (EIN) (used for income tax forms, it is similar to an individual's social security number)
  - Federal unemployment (Form 940)
  - Income tax withholding, social security, Medicare (Form 941)

- Employee income tax reporting (W-2)
- Employer summary of W-2s (W-3)
- Employee withholding form (W-4)
- Employee proof of citizenship (I-9)
- Dividend or similar payments (1099) (actually, at last count, there are 16 different 1099 forms)

- *State government*

  Each state has its own forms and regulations; following is a general list:

  - State unemployment
  - State income tax withholding
  - Worker's compensation (they call it insurance, but in reality it's a tax)
  - New hire reporting
  - Sales and use tax: state, county, city, stadium
  - Professional licenses (architect, surveyor, landscape architect, and engineer, to mention a few)
  - Work permits for employees under the age of 18

Fringe Benefits

Providing fringe benefits to employees, including owners, requires additional paperwork and reporting. This is an area where it is very important to work closely with your lawyer and accountant. The rules and regulations covering fringe benefits are complex and difficult to decipher. Three of the most common fringe benefits are (1) use of a company owned vehicle, (2) retirement plans such as 401(k) and SIMPLE IRA, and (3) medical reimbursement plans. Each is governed by its own Internal Revenue Service rulings. Business owners should be aware of each ruling, how it may affect taxable income, and what type of record keeping is required.

An employee may use a company vehicle for personal use, including daily commuting; however, the value of the personal use is included as taxable income for the employee. An employee who uses a company vehicle must keep records that substantiate the portion spent for personal use.

Optional retirement plans have become much easier to administer in recent years. Typically, an

Tip...

Smart Tip

Get a copy of IRS Publication 15-B, which covers employee fringe benefits. Pay particular attention to the sections that cover "highly compensated employees" who may be ineligible for some tax-free benefits.

35

employee elects to have a portion of his pay deducted and invested in a mutual fund or other investment. Usually the company matches the employee's contribution up to a limit set by the IRS. Depending on the type of retirement plan, the amount contributed may be deducted from the employee's taxable income; the company's contribution is generally tax free.

Medical reimbursement plans are not as widely known as retirement plans, but can offer tremendous benefits. Essentially, a company may reimburse an employee for medical expenses that are not covered by health insurance. In this case, the IRS has created a list of medical services that are covered under the program. Payments to employees as reimbursements are not recorded as taxable income as long as all full-time employees, those who work at least 35 hours per week for more than nine months, are covered by the plan and the company has a written policy explaining it. If a company does not wish to administer the plan itself, it can hire an insurance company to do it.

Documentation and Receipts

All around the country, businesses have warehouses full of boxes of receipts, cancelled checks, invoices, and government forms. New technology has helped somewhat as computers can store an incredible amount of information. However, in most cases, it is necessary to have a paper trail to back up the computer data. According to the IRS, a business must retain records for "as long as they may be needed for the administration of any provision of the Internal Revenue Code." Don't forget that the Code has nearly 17,000 pages. Fortunately the IRS does give some guidance on this issue on its web site; as long as the business does not file fraudulent reports, most records can be discarded after seven years.

State governments have their own set of record-keeping guidelines. For example, the Wisconsin Department of Revenue Sales Tax Division routinely audits businesses to ensure that they are collecting and remitting the proper amount of tax. Its audit usually covers four years; however, it can request records for earlier years if it finds fraudulent activity during the initial audit period.

Record-keeping is also useful to a business for its own internal uses. As mentioned earlier, keeping records related to employee benefits is of utmost importance. These items are often red flags for government auditors; a well-organized

Tip...

Smart Tip
Proof of payment of an amount, by itself, does not establish you are entitled to a tax deduction. You should also keep other documents, such as credit card slips, invoices, and employee time cards to show that you also incurred the cost.

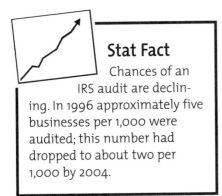

Stat Fact

Chances of an IRS audit are declining. In 1996 approximately five businesses per 1,000 were audited; this number had dropped to about two per 1,000 by 2004.

set of records documenting and justifying benefits will usually save a company time and money in the event of an audit.

Employee performance records are also important because segments of the contracting industry have fairly high turnover of employees and relatively high rates for unemployment compensation. An employee who is fired or laid off is usually eligible to receive unemployment benefits; if an employee is fired because of violations of company policy, he may be ineligible for benefits. However, in order for denial of benefits, the employer must keep a written record of the violations of company policy. These may include unexcused absences, repeated tardiness, or failure to follow safety procedures. Chapter 9 covers the importance of an employee handbook that sets out company policy.

The best approach to record keeping is to be prepared for the audit that may never come. The actual chances of being audited by the IRS are slim. However, it is better to be safe than sorry because audits are very time consuming and can be an expensive. The good news is that one audit department rarely passes information learned from an audit to another branch of government. For example, a number of years ago a new business owner paid himself by dividends rather than a salary. He was audited by the Social Security Administration which determined that the income he received was actually wages, not dividends. It charged him the appropriate social security and Medicare taxes; however, it did not inform the IRS or the state revenue department of what had been found.

Most businesses can, however, expect an annual audit by their Worker's Compensation Insurance Carrier. This compulsory insurance protects employees against loss of income and supplies medical payments if they are hurt on the job. Because the premiums are based on total payroll, the insurance companies perform an audit every year. Be sure to correctly record employee overtime costs; a portion is exempt from worker's compensation. Therefore, a business owner must keep records of payroll for each job classification in the organization. Failure to keep accurate records can result in overpayment of premiums; for example, recent rates in Wisconsin were $0.29 per $100 of

Dollar Stretcher

Some states exempt very small employers from carrying worker's compensation; other states exempt owners who hold more than 25 percent of the stock of the company. Other states cap the amount of income of owners that is taxed. Learn the regulations, and save yourself some money.

wages for office workers, while landscape workers' rates approach $11.50 per $100 of wages.

Chapter 4 Highlights

★ The business structure you select will have an important impact on the amount of taxes you pay, the amount of personal risk you assume, and the level of control you have over your business. Careful consideration, in consultation with your lawyer and accountant, must be made prior to choosing a legal structure.

★ The "Government" may seem like a huge monster lurking in the shadows waiting to pounce on the unsuspecting business owner. However, with careful organization and proper accounting, it is relatively easy to satisfy the requirements of both state and federal governments. Ignorance of the law is no excuse for violating the rules.

★ Almost everyone dislikes paperwork. However, maintaining good records is critical to all business enterprises. It is far better to be prepared for the government or insurance audit that may never come; the alternative is usually time wasted trying to locate documents or, failing that, additional costs resulting from incorrect reporting to these agencies.

It's Moving Day

Those of you who watch professional golf tournaments on television have, undoubtedly, heard the commentators refer to the third day of the tournament (usually Saturday) as "moving day." Golf tournaments typically run four consecutive days, Thursday through Sunday. After the first two days, the field of players is reduced by about one-half; those with the highest scores do not advance to play on the weekend. For the successful players, the first two days are spent playing well enough to "make the cut." Once the cut is made, the focus turns to scoring low and winning the most money possible. On "moving day," players try to position themselves to have a chance of actually winning the tournament. They figure that, depending on the quality of the competition and the difficulty of the golf course, if they can get within five or six shots of the leader they have a chance to win.

So here we are in Chapter 5, Moving Day, the time to make the big step toward success. At this point, entrepreneurs should have a clear understanding of the basic foundation needed to start a business:

Dollar Stretcher

State government has a significant influence on businesses. Some states encourage business formation and tailor their taxes to appeal to business. Others implement tax policies that are unfriendly to business. The five most business-friendly states are Wyoming, South Dakota, Alaska, Nevada, and Florida; the least friendly are Vermont, New York, New Jersey, Ohio, and at the very bottom, Rhode Island.

- They understand what a contracting business is and why it is important to the community and the economy.
- They know if they have the proper background, credentials, and personality to become successful.
- They have carefully researched and prepared a business plan and know how they will finance their enterprise.
- They have established relationships with and have consulted with their lawyer, accountant, banker, and insurance agent.
- They understand the requirements that must be met to satisfy state and federal government agencies. They've obtained the licenses they need and have established the required government accounts.

Open Your Office and Shop

One of the first questions start-up business owners ask themselves is, "Where should I set up my operations and how much space do I need?" Many start in their own homes, either in the basement or a spare room. There are certain advantages to starting this way but also many problems.

The positive aspects are largely related to costs. It's cheap. The structure is already there so you have no initial costs to construct or rent a building. You may have some remodeling to do, but most often this can be done at a reasonable cost. There are no rental expenses to pay every month and no landlord to deal with. It's also very convenient to have your office at your home; no time is wasted commuting. Property maintenance and utility costs can be shared by the home owner (you) and your business. Finally, home improvement expenses such as a new roof can, in part, be treated as a business expense.

Now for the downside: The Internal Revenue Service has very strict rules regarding in-home offices; some accountants believe that having an in-home office increases the chances of a tax audit. Once again, it is better to prepare for the audit that will probably never come. Follow the letter of the law; use your office for business purposes only, keep meticulous records of your expenses, draw a scaled plan of your home with the office portion clearly outlined, and take photographs to support the drawings.

Family support is a crucial factor in deciding to run your business from your home. Because you can never really get away from the office, it's easy to spend too much time at work. Imagine saying to your spouse or partner, "Honey, I'm just going downstairs for half an hour and organize the files for the Smith job." Three hours later, after filing the Smith papers, the Jones papers, and the Anderson papers; sending e-mails to suppliers ordering materials for the jobs; and talking on the telephone to three prospective clients, you climb the stairs to find a fuming spouse and a cold dinner. Remember in Chapter 2 when I talked about the importance of good time management? It applies to your family as well as your clients and employees—even more so when you have the office in your home.

There are other things to think about when considering a home office. It's important to be able to have a normal home life as well as a stimulating and successful business environment. Ask yourself these questions before you open an office in your home:

- Do you have employees who will work full time in your home? How does your spouse or partner feel about it?
- Do you expect to meet with clients at your home? If you do not have a separate entrance to your office, how do your spouse and children feel about strangers walking through their home?
- Will the neighbors complain about increased truck traffic stopping to deliver supplies? Will they be happy if you have several trucks and vans parked in your driveway each night?
- Do you have enough space to store all you equipment and supplies?
- Will your young children interfere with the business? Will they be safe?
- Do local zoning codes allow business activity in your neighborhood?

Space: The Next Frontier

No matter where you ultimately decide to open up shop, you must decide how much space you'll need to operate efficiently. As is usually the case, when you think you have just the perfect size office, it will instantly become too small. Ideally, an office should be designed with some flexibility. Most businesses add staff over time and need space for each individual to perform his duties. At a minimum, contractors should have space for the owner, the staff, and a meeting room.

The office for the chief executive of the company should be large enough to hold meetings with at least several people; an area 12 by 12 is a suggested minimum. Individual staff members such as an office manager, bookkeeper, sales staff, and estimator should have spaces ranging in size from 6 by 6 to 8 by 8. These spaces are large enough for a desk, computer, filing cabinet, and perhaps a comfortable chair.

The work space for design staff should be determined by the equipment they use. The drafting table is rapidly becoming a relic as most new designers and architects work on a personal computer. However, they may need space for a plotter to print out plans, and a table to lay them out. Storage space for the printed designs is critical and usually takes up lots of space.

A small conference or meeting room for meeting with clients and sales representatives or holding staff meetings is essential to many businesses in the contracting industry. Some interior designers have suggested that meeting rooms should be designed so that each person attending the meeting has 30 to 35 square feet of space; therefore, if you anticipate meetings with two to six people, a room 12 by 16 should be adequate.

Storage space is often overlooked when planning a new office. Office supplies, machinery, and financial data archives take up quite a bit of room. In addition, most offices have spaces for coffee makers, microwave ovens, and book shelves for industry-specific publications.

Office Specifications and Details

Now that you've got a place for your stuff, you have to decide what that stuff is. A well-stocked and organized office runs much smoother and more successfully than one in a continual state of disarray. If good organization is not a strong suit of a contractor-owner, then she should consider hiring an experienced office manager or executive assistant to keep the office and support staff working smoothly and efficiently. Some of the physical items every contracting office should have are the following.

Communications I

The ability to communicate clearly and promptly with both co-workers and clients is critical to a contracting business, so the first order of business is installing a telephone system that meets the needs of the business. Even a one-person shop should have two incoming telephone land lines so that potential clients rarely get a busy signal when calling to inquire about services and prices. Initially, a single answering machine with a professionally delivered greeting is adequate for a new contracting business. As the business grows, more lines are necessary not only to handle the increased volume of calls but also to make sure that messages from clients are channeled properly. Many local telephone companies offer a voice mailbox that will record messages if all the incoming lines are busy.

Ultimately, as an office evolves, a PBX (public branch exchange) system may be necessary. These sophisticated systems, usually costing several thousand dollars, provide a network within an office that offers automatic answering, call transfer, individual voice mail, intercom systems, conference calling, and the ability to forward calls to another location. Typically, these systems offer callers menu options for their calls: by pressing a series of numbers, the caller can be transferred directly to the person or department sought.

While a PBX telephone system increases the efficiency and usually the professional image of a company, care must be used when relying on one. Many potential clients are turned away by menu options; most people like to speak with a "real live person" and become impatient or angry when forced to listen to a long list of instructions and options. Everyone has made telephone calls that ended up in a seemingly never-ending loop: The target of the call remained elusive, and the opportunity to speak with a real person seemed a bleak possibility at best. The most successful companies endeavor to answer each call personally and rely on the automatic answer functions as a backup, at night, or over the weekend. Because the first call a potential client makes is often his introduction to the company, the method of greeting is crucial. A poor first impression can easily turn away potential clients. Both the real live person and the answering machine should have a pleasant, professional voice that is easily understood, and calls should be transferred quickly and correctly. Good salespeople often say, "If I can just get my foot in the door, I know I can make the sale." Similarly, a professional method of answering the telephone can go a long way help make the sale.

Communications II

While cellular or mobile telephones have been in existence since the 1940s, it was not until the late 1980s or early 1990s that they began to grow in popularity. Early telephones were cumbersome "bag phones" that only worked when they were plugged into a cigarette lighter in an automobile or truck. As technology improved, cell phone use grew astronomically. Today, these telephones work almost anywhere in the world, are extremely small, and do much more than merely make a telephone call. Around the world, approximately one in three people owns a cell phone; and according to CTIA, the wireless association, the number of cell phone users in the United States has climbed to over two-thirds of the population.

Cell phones are valuable tools for businesses of all sizes. At the typical mom and pop contracting company, the owner is typically on a job site all day, every day; often telephone service is not available. At various times over the course of a day or week, the owner must be able to communicate with clients to ensure that work is proceeding properly, with the office for a wide variety of reasons, with suppliers to verify deliveries or order materials, with future clients to schedule meetings, and with an architect or designer to ask questions about the work.

Larger companies also rely on cell phones to coordinate work among several work crews; perhaps a piece of machinery has to be shared by two crews or machinery breaks and a replacement is needed. If the owner is not present on the job site, the cell phone is an invaluable tool for the crew foreman to verify details of an installation or get approval for changing the plans. Finally, the cell phone is a safety tool. In the event of a serious injury on the job, medical help can be called and the injured worker treated without unnecessary delay.

Cellular telephone service is very competitive and in a constant state of change. Internet web sites such as www.wirelessguide.org and www.myrateplan.com are valuable

---

Phone Facts

The first telephone, invented by Alexander Graham Bell in 1876, was called an "electric speech machine." The first automatic answering machine was built in 1935 and was three feet tall. It wasn't until 1956 that the very first transatlantic telephone call was made from Scotland to Nova Scotia. (Radio telephone calls had been made many years earlier.) Touch-tone dialing began to replace rotary dialing in 1963. On July 20, 1969, President Richard Nixon used the telephone in the Oval Office at the White House to call Apollo 11 astronauts Neil Armstrong and Buzz Aldrin while they were exploring the moon. Cordless telephones made their first appearance about 1980 and offered very limited range and poor sound quality; 1990 brought improved cordless phones but at a cost of nearly $400. The fax machine was actually invented in 1843 by Alexander Bain, but did not become widely used until the late 1980s.

tools for learning about the cell phone plans available in various regions of the country. However, it is always better to speak personally with a sales representative who specializes in the needs of businesses. A company that needs several cellular telephones can often negotiate a better price by talking with a salesperson.

Communications III

Getting the idea? Efficient communications systems are the lifeblood of any business. Every office needs the following machines to streamline communications and make running the business more efficient, and inevitably, more successful:

1. *Telephone answering machine.* Unless your office has a PBX system, this works. While it is preferable to have a real person answer calls, an answering machine is a useful tool for times when the office staff is busy and for evening and weekends.

2. *Fax machine.* It's useful for ordering materials, sending government and insurance reports, sending and receiving client documents such as proposals and change orders, and ordering office supplies.

3. *Copy machine.* It's invaluable for making duplicate records, printing copies of inter-office memos for distribution, and a myriad of other uses too numerous to mention.

4. *Multi-function machine.* It can do many of the above tasks from a single source. These versatile machines can be connected to a personal computer and print, scan, fax, and copy documents of all types; they can also be used as stand-alone machines and act as your primary copy machine.

Computers

The personal computer became an invaluable business tool in the late 1980s. Most contracting businesses have at least one computer, and many have several. Not only can computers be used for creating and saving word processing documents and mathematical spreadsheets, they have also revolutionized the accounting functions of small business.

A simple desktop computer can handle the daily work of the business. A more powerful computer is needed for Computer Aided Drafting (CAD) work. A laptop (notebook) computer can be a useful selling tool, with photographs of completed work available to show prospective clients.

Accounting software from companies like QuickBooks and Peachtree allow a company to streamline and organize its payroll, accounts payable, accounts receivable, and income and balance sheets. In addition, these software packages can help organize inventory, track job costs, as well as prepare a wide variety of reports needed for government reporting and for monitoring the financial status of the business.

Much to the dismay of some older architects and designers, the computer has replaced the drafting board and T-square as the primary tool for designing property development projects. Not only do computers make it much easier to make changes and revisions to plans, they can create cost estimates for clients and share information with other design or installation professionals.

Finally, connecting the computer to the World Wide Web via the internet has become the modern way of advertising, communicating, and purchasing. There are, however, several cautionary notes about using the computer as a business tool. First, data and information can be lost if the computer breaks down or is damaged by an electrical storm. Therefore, it is critically important to have a good backup program to save records. Indeed, most computer consultants recommend using two sets of backup media such as the CD, DVD, or external hard drive and a third back up that is taken off-site and kept in a secure place. (Just imagine the difficulties created if your building burns down and all your in-house backups are destroyed.) Second, computers are vulnerable to a wide variety of viruses that can either disrupt normal operations or, in the worst case, steal vital information such as bank account or social security numbers. And, third, employers must be on the alert for employees who use the computer for personal or illicit purposes.

> **Fun Fact**
>
> During the early 1950s, the first commercial computer built in the United States, named UNIVAC, occupied more than 350 square feet of office space (about the size of a 2-car garage) and had the ability to perform 1,900 operations per second. In 2006, IBM built a much smaller supercomputer named BlueGene/L capable of performing 280,600,000,000,000 calculations per second.

Office Supplies

Every office needs everyday supplies. Use the Office Supplies Checklist on pages 47–48 to help you stock the useful items you'll need to equip your office. Use this list to also help you set up a reasonable budget for your office.

Tools and Equipment

The contracting industry is large and diverse; each segment has its own specialized tools and equipment. Some contractors work most efficiently when they carry their equipment in a van, some need dump trucks, while others rely on pickup trucks with specialized compartments and racks. The same is true for power and hand tools. The best advice I can give is to talk with other contractors and ask what they use. Many established, successful contractors are more than happy to help a fledgling business get started. Another approach is to stop at job sites and see what other contractors use;

Office Supplies Checklist

Use this handy list as a shopping guide for equipping your office with supplies (you probably already have some of these). After you've done your shopping, fill in the purchase price next to each item, add up your costs, and you'll have a head start on estimating your start-up costs. Of course, this is not a complete list of supplies that you may need, so tailor it to what you think you will use.

Items	Price
❏ Postage scale	$_____
❏ Postage meter or stamps	$_____
❏ Paper for fax machine and copy machine	$_____
❏ Toner and ink cartridges for fax machine, copy machine, and computer printer	$_____
❏ "Sticky" notes in an assortment of sizes	$_____
❏ Scratch and telephone message pads	$_____
❏ Waste baskets	$_____
❏ Scissors, Exacto® knives, staplers	$_____
❏ Three-ring binders and file folders	$_____
❏ Drafting tools: pencils, sharpeners, erasers, scales, templates, French curves, tracing paper, paper rolls for plotter, masking tape	$_____
❏ Envelopes and stationery with your logo/company name	$_____
❏ Return envelopes with your address preprinted	$_____
❏ Wall safe for storing valuable papers, cash, and computer backup disks	$_____
❏ Time clock and cards	$_____
❏ Digital camera	$_____
❏ Measuring wheel and 100-foot tape measure	$_____
❏ Marking paint and long-handled paint gun	$_____
❏ Business cards	$_____
❏ Surge protectors for computers	$_____
❏ Calculators	$_____
❏ Calendars and/or planners	$_____

Office Supplies Checklist, continued

- ❏ CD and/or DVD disks $ _____
- ❏ Desk organizers $ _____
- ❏ Office furniture: desks, chairs, chair mats, file cabinets, conference table and chairs, computer work stations, lamps, shelving $ _____
- ❏ Fire extinguishers and first aid kit $ _____
- ❏ Coffee machine and microwave (optional) $ _____
- ❏ Paper punch $ _____
- ❏ Janitorial and bathroom supplies $ _____

Total Office Supplies Expenditures: $ _____

of course if you have been an employee of a contractor and are striking out on your own, you already know which tools and equipment you'll need to get started.

Necessary Intangibles

In addition to the tangible items mentioned above, a business owner must be aware of several supplemental or "intangible" items he should have to operate his business legally and efficiently. Dealing with the law and the G-Man may not be an enticing prospect, but the penalties for ignoring them can be severe and devastating.

The Bureaucracy

In Chapter 4, I discussed the types of governmental and insurance accounts required of most businesses. Below is a supplemental list of items and accounts each business should have. Much of this information can be found on the internet at www.business.gov.

- *Labor law posters.* These are required by both the federal and state governments. These explain various rules and regulations established by government agencies such as the Equal Employment Opportunity Commission (EEOC). These posters, which must be placed in an area where all employees can easily read them, can be ordered from government organizations or from the U.S. Department of Labor. Private companies sell all-in-one posters that include all the required information. Some of these include only federal government posters, others cover individual states, and some are a combination of federal and specific state information.

- *Occupational Safety and Health Administration (OSHA) Form 300.* Log of work-related injury and illness.
- *OSHA Form 301.* Injury and illness incident report.
- *OSHA Form 300A.* Summary of work-related injury and illness. This report must be filled out and posted where employees can read it even if there are no reported work-related injuries or illnesses.
- *Material Safety Data Sheets (MSDS).* Forms that contain information and data about chemicals and other hazardous substances. The forms contain instructions for safe use of a material and procedures for dealing with emergencies. Employers must have the sheets available for employees who may come in contact with hazardous materials. Suppliers of these materials usually provide the sheets upon request.
- *Minor's work permit.* Employees under 18 years old must obtain a work permit prior to starting their employment. These workers have limitations placed on them based on their age and the type of work they perform. Both federal and state regulations apply to these workers. Contractors must be very careful when hiring young employees because strict safety regulations apply to minor workers. For example, young workers can neither operate a circular saw nor even assist operations that use a circular saw. These employees may not work as roofers. Other regulations govern maximum work hours allowed both on a daily and weekly basis and strict limitations on driving vehicles and operating machinery.

Credit Cards

Be very careful with using credit cards. Failure to pay the full amount due each and every month is an extremely expensive mistake. When late fees are added to interest charges, the cost of paying only a portion of the monthly invoice can easily exceed 20 percent of your purchases. Using a credit card can be a very useful tool for a company. However, care should be taken when deciding which employees have the authority to have or use one. The best advice is to keep the list of users to a bare minimum and require that itemized receipts accompany the monthly invoice and each purchase has a legitimate business purpose.

Supplier Credit

Positive cash flow is often a problem for new businesses. During a project, funds are spent on wages and materials. Many times a client is not presented an invoice for the work until completion of the project and then may wait 30 days, or longer, to pay the bill. By securing credit with suppliers, a contractor can ease the pressure on cash flow—the money that comes in and out of the bank account. If managed properly, a contractor can purchase materials and often pay for them 30 to 60 days later. While some suppliers request payment in ten days, most do not charge a late fee until the invoice is more than 30 days past due. Every effort must be made to pay supplier invoices on time; and when cash is tight and payments cannot be made on time, the contractor must contact the supplier and explain the situation. Most suppliers are cooperative, especially if the contractor has a good payment record. Still, there are other suppliers who "go by the book" and do not agree to the delay of payment; some will even send a notice to your client that they will place a lien on his property if payment is not made. For obvious reasons, contractors must avoid this scenario at all cost.

> **⚠ Beware!**
>
> A construction, or mechanic's, lien is used to collect past due amounts owed to a company claiming the lien. These liens can be attached to land, buildings, or partially completed new construction. Once a lien is placed on property, the owner may lose some control over it until the lien has been satisfied and the past due amounts paid in full. Lien laws vary widely from one state to another and can be very complicated. Understanding how the lien law works in your state may save you money, time, and embarrassment.

Banking

Most contracting businesses require at least two types of bank accounts for handling their cash: a checking account, which does not pay interest, for accounts payable and payroll, and a savings or money market account for holding excess cash until it is needed. Interest rates for these types of accounts vary and change as the national economy changes.

Using cash as a vehicle to pay suppliers or employees is a very poor way to do business; doing so makes record-keeping difficult and opens the door to abuse and even theft. Instead, checks, credit, and credit cards are far better and safer methods of spending money. A recent and helpful innovation is online banking. Here accounts can be monitored and bills paid using the internet. Use online banking only if your own accounting software is compatible with the your bank's system.

Start Me Up

Many entrepreneurs start their own business because they do not want to work at repetitive or boring jobs. Factory work has no appeal to them. They cannot imagine sitting behind a desk eight hours a day shuffling papers. Spending days in a retail store is abhorrent to their senses. They are looking for work that is not routine and varies from day to day. The contracting industry offers just the type of working atmosphere that these entrepreneurs want and enjoy.

If you were to ask a contractor to describe a typical day at work, he would tell you that there is no such thing. That's not to say that each of the 60 or 70 hours you will work each week are thrilling and rewarding. Every job has its unpleasant moments, and the contracting industry is no exception. However, for a vast majority of successful contractors, the fun times on the job far outnumber the frustrating and unpleasant times.

Most contractors begin their day well before 7 A.M. when they begin to review the schedule for the day. While they usually have a schedule for the week (refer to Chapter 2, Sample Work Schedule), disruption and change are the norm. What are some of the causes for changing the schedule at the last minute? Here are a few to explain why contractors must remain flexible:

- Poor weather can cause a situation where even if you can get onto the job site, your work would not be productive.
- An employee calls in sick.
- Supplies ordered for a job have been delayed in shipment.
- The supplier has sent the wrong materials.
- Equipment breakdown; a spare is not available.
- The client has changed his mind and wants to review the plans before more work is done.
- A subcontractor has not completed her work or has to alter work already completed.

The top entrepreneurs appear to have an instinctive ability to "see the big picture" and understand that the various elements of their business must work harmoniously for the business to succeed. However, the importance of attending to the smallest detail cannot be stressed enough. Entrepreneurs who are able to set effective company policies and passionately communicate their vision for success but overlook or ignore seemingly mundane details, such as meeting financial deadlines or following through on promises to employees or customers, are likely heading down the road to failure. This is not to imply that owners should micro-manage their business, but must convey the importance of "attention to detail" to their employees.

Many new contractors wear multiple hats. They are the employer, the workforce, the scheduler, the mechanic, the designer, the bookkeeper, and the salesperson. While a spouse or partner may be of great assistance with these tasks, the owner usually has to spend a portion of his day on one or more of these tasks. Orders for materials have to be reviewed, customer statements have to be verified, equipment must be maintained, and new business secured. Most often, a contractor will work in the field during the day, spend a few hours in the late afternoon or early evening meeting with prospective clients, and then head back to the office to take care of paperwork and make telephone calls.

Saturdays are much the same, except more time may be spent on equipment maintenance, paperwork, and communications with clients. The weekend typically becomes Saturday night and all day Sunday. With disruption and chaos constantly lurking in the background, it is vital that contractors remain flexible enough to "change horses in midstream" and be nimble enough to remain productive when the expected work schedule is changed. One of the keys to success for contractors is to learn how to efficiently schedule your labor and to manage the productivity of your work crews. It makes no difference if you are a one-person outfit or have 30 employees; productivity of labor must be constantly maintained even when all or some of the factors listed above are threatening to bring your workday to a screeching halt.

A contractor does not generate income for every hour he or she works. Time spent on the telephone or calling on a prospective client is not what some lawyers call "billable hours." Contractors rarely can send a bill to client who calls to ask questions about her project; time spent preparing government reports cannot be billed to anyone. In Chapter 6, you will learn about budgeting and how to get paid for the hours when actual income is not being generated.

The contractor must become something of a juggler when family or personal situations arise that require absence from work. Your teenage son's championship soccer game is scheduled for 3 P.M. on Thursday; your daughter is starring in the school play scheduled for 1 P.M. on Wednesday; your spouse wants you to take the kids away for a few days to the new water park; your doctor has scheduled some tests for 9 A.M. Monday morning. For the very small contractor, these obligations do not pose a huge problem. Many clients understand that contractors actually have lives besides their work and are agreeable when you inform them in advance that you'll not be on the job during those hours. But you must remember that during these times you are not generating income; while you may pay yourself a weekly salary from the business, you are not generating the income to pay that salary if you are not working.

Missing work is more difficult for the medium-sized contractor who has just a few employees. When you take time off to tend to personal obligations, your field workers may be left without proper supervision. Therefore, proper planning for the productivity of your work crew becomes a critical issue. Before an owner can send a field employee to a job site unsupervised, she must be confident that the employee has the knowledge and ability to complete the tasks satisfactorily. As some employees learn faster than others, the owner must be able to take whatever time is necessary to properly train each individual.

'Tis the Season

Some specialties in the contracting industry face unique challenges as a result of geographical location and weather. In the southwestern regions of the United States, extreme heat during the summer may limit the amount of physical activity that workers should do. Many who live there might say "It's hot, but it's dry heat." However, if it is 115 degrees, it's still hot. Employees working under these conditions should receive training to limit the risks of working in hot weather, to recognize the symptoms of the onset of heat exhaustion or heat stroke, and to learn what steps they should take if they or a co-worker becomes disabled due to heat stroke.

In other areas of the country, particularly in the north, contractors face obstacles created by adverse weather during the winter months. When the ground is frozen, excavators, landscape contractors, and even plumbers may not be able to work on a consistent basis. Some may have to lay off employees and reduce their staff to a bare minimum.

In recent years, however, many of these northern businesses have offered new services in order to maintain a revenue stream. Two of the most popular are snow removal and holiday decorating. Some have sold Christmas trees. I've even heard of one contractor who provides carpet cleaning services during the winter and another, an excavator, who keeps busy repairing snowmobiles.

Innovative entrepreneurs consider all their options, examine the costs and benefits they expect from a new venture, weigh the strengths and weaknesses of their staff, and forge ahead with the new service. Clients will expect the same high level of performance that is provided by your regular services. Therefore, employees must be properly trained to perform the tasks required by the seasonal service; substandard work will backfire and hurt the reputation of the company as a whole.

Chapter 5 Highlights

* Using your home as an office can be very beneficial to a new contracting business; however, there are disadvantages.
* Plan your spatial needs before building or renting; most likely, you'll need more space than you think.
* Up-to-date communications systems are crucial to the success of a new contracting business.
* Set a realistic and thorough budget for office supplies and equipment.
* Visit www.business.gov to learn about the variety of government regulations that cover small business.

★ Visit your state's web site to discover relevant regulations.

★ There is no such thing as a typical day in the contracting industry.

★ Geographical location may bring special challenges to many contracting businesses.

Budgets and Estimates

Financial Techniques for Profitability

Some business owners suffer from irregular heart palpitations at the prospect of facing the law or the G-man. However, this terror is actually fairly infrequent and, when it does happen, usually more annoying than threatening.

However, when it comes to financial matters, many contractors simply put on blinders, preferring to practice their craft rather than manage their money and finances. They would do well to remember Benjamin Franklin, who wisely said:

Beware of small expenses;
a small leak will sink a great ship.

While there are numerous reasons why businesses fail, accounting issues rank near the top for companies engaged in contracting. Many contractors fail to correctly recognize their true cost of doing business and thus fail to properly price their services. It is very interesting to know that in the same geographical area of the country, competitive bids for the same work from several contractors can differ by as much as 30 percent. Does this mean that some contractors deliberately overcharge their clients or that others are giving the work away? Absolutely not. There are legitimate reasons for a wide variance among bids for the same work. Contractor A, for example, may have a larger, more stable, and more experienced workforce who demand higher wages, while contractor B may work out of his home, have few employees, and thus have very low expenses. However, contractor C may not truly understand and account for all of his expenses and therefore actually undercharge clients.

Contractors who have a reputation for excellent work that is completed on time and within budget are usually able to charge more than the contractor who is late, installs the incorrect product, and adds "extra charges" when the project is completed. This chapter covers the strategies for establishing a budget and using it to calculate a fair and profitable price for services. It establishes the framework for Chapter 7, which explains how to use the budget to determine what level of annual revenues is needed to make a profit.

The Tools to Make a Budget

Creating a budget for a new contracting business can be a difficult because of the lack of a spending history. Established businesses have years of spending records to help them estimate future spending. Without a track record, a new business must make educated projections based on the best available information and then actively monitor and update its budget as actual spending information is known.

Assistance may be available from a number of sources, including former employers, industry associations, suppliers, and even some competitors. Asking a large competitor for help might seem like a daunting task, but surprisingly, many large, established companies are eager to help a start-up contracting business. They take it as a compliment that someone respects them enough to ask for advice. They have a vested interest in seeing that new businesses in their industry present themselves in a

Dollar Stretcher

Most software companies offer product upgrades nearly every year. Often, these upgrades offer minor changes to the basic programming. While it is important to keep up to date with the latest software enhancements, money can be saved by upgrading your software *every other time it is offered*. Study the new features offered by an upgrade and decide if you can postpone them by a year or so. Caution: if your software becomes obsolete because you skipped too many upgrades, it's probable that the software company will cease providing technical support for your older software.

positive light. And, they are so well established that they have few worries about competition from a start-up.

But what is the contractor-entrepreneur to do with the information gained from learning about the spending habits of other businesses in the contracting industry? Several items are critical, with the first being, for obvious reasons, a computer with an internet connection. Even the smallest businesses benefit from using a computer in their business because of the amount of information that can be stored on a computer and the speed at which data can be compiled and organized. While the computer and the internet can be used to purchase materials and supplies, compose text documents, and assist with project design, accounting and mathematical functions are at the top of the list for most contractors.

Gone are the days of the lowly clerk, perched at a corner desk for endless hours with pencil and eraser in hand, transcribing columns of numbers, cross adding and crosschecking until all the sums come out correctly. It was even worse when the task fell to the owner or her spouse. Fortunately this tedious but extremely important work has been replaced by a variety of accounting software programs that offer freedom from the burdens of day-to-day financial management. These programs provide contractors with the tools to manage their business and their employees, streamline their operations, and offer a variety of solutions for nearly every financial need a small business has. By using accounting software, a contractor can track expenses, both by category and by supplier; organize client information and accounts receivable; manage employee wages, deductions, and benefits; and accurately file government reports and payments. Three of the most popular accounting programs for small business are Peachtree Complete by Sage Software Inc. (www.peachtree.com), MYOB Business Essentials Pro by MYOB (www.myob-us.com), and QuickBooks Pro by Intuit, Inc. (www.intuit.com).

There is another invaluable tool that becomes the heart of the budget-making process—the spreadsheet. In 1978, a Harvard student named Dan Bricklin conceived of an electronic spreadsheet while one of his professors was creating a financial model using chalk on the blackboard. When the professor found an error during the lesson, he had to erase and rewrite a number of sequential entries. When Bricklin developed his computer-based spreadsheet, which he named VisiCalc, he could change one incorrect entry in a series, and the remainder of the numbers in the series would change automatically. VisiCalc is generally credited with changing computer use from a hobby to a valuable business tool. While there are many spreadsheets available, including some available free over the internet, the most recognizable and widely-used is Excel, produced by Microsoft Corporation.

As you will learn later in this chapter, the spreadsheet is helpful with financial management because it can be used to understand the effects of increased or decreased spending. For example, the spreadsheet can be used to answer a question like, "If I hire a salesperson and increase total wages by $25,000, how much will the cost of employee benefits increase and how much more revenue will I need to generate this year to pay for these increased costs? OK, now what happens if the person I hire wants to be paid $35,000?" All the budget maker has to do is enter either amount of the new wage, and the questions will be automatically answered. It's a great tool for all sorts of "what-if" questions.

Why Set a Budget?

Establishing a budget for your business is a key ingredient to success. A contracting company may have the most skilled employees, the newest equipment, a top-notch sales team, and a creative advertising program; but failure is destined if the company does not have a comprehensive financial plan. The budget is the first step in creating this plan and offers the following benefits:

- Helps plan for the future
- Helps plan and manage your money
- Helps identify problems before they occur or get out of hand
- Helps you meet your goals and objectives
- Improves the decision-making process
- Increases employee motivation
- Helps keep costs under control
- Monitors performance on a variety of levels.

Smart Tip

When establishing a budget, weigh the costs and benefits of your spending decisions. For example, let's say you plan to buy a piece of equipment for $10,000. However, the dealer has another model that is larger, faster, and more efficient at a cost of $14,000. Ask yourself if the additional cost of $4,000 will generate a net benefit to the company of *at least* that much. If it does, buy the more expensive model. This concept of marginalism shows that additional (marginal) costs and additional (marginal) benefits are pertinent to financial decision making.

Although the budget can be considered a road map to financial success, the way is littered with potholes and detours. Never consider your budget to be a fixed document that you prepare once and never change. It is a dynamic document that will undergo revisions and modifications during the year. Most often, these changes will be minor, with little effect on your overall financial plan.

Costs First

Many new business owners begin their budget process by trying to determine what their total revenues will be for the year. They think that by considering revenues first, they'll be in a position to know how much money they can spend during the course of the year. What they often overlook is consideration of how they will achieve the projected revenues. Merely knowing or guessing annual revenues does not provide a strategy for pricing your services nor does it instill any kind of spending discipline.

The budget process begins and ends with a detailed and organized system that projects annual spending in various categories and then uses these spending amounts to determine the amount of revenue needed to pay for the spending, leaving enough at the end of the year for a profit.

Direct Costs

The sample budget used in this chapter will be divided into three distinct categories of expenses, each with its own unique characteristics. The first category contains direct job costs, or just direct costs, expenses specifically related to projects completed by the company. Specifically, it includes materials, labor, and subcontractors, if any; it also includes the rental of any equipment that might be required to complete the projects.

One of the most difficult concepts for new contractor-owners to grasp is the true cost of labor. An employee earning $10 per hour actually costs his or her employer much more than that. In addition to the hourly wage, the employer incurs costs in the following categories:

- Social security and Medicare taxes
- Unemployment taxes, both federal and state
- Worker's compensation insurance
- Paid holidays and vacations; sick days
- Health insurance premiums
- Overtime

When you combine these costs, which I call the "labor burden," you'll get a truer picture of your actual cost of doing business. Most businesses have different classes of employees such as the field laborers who install the projects, the sales force, and the office staff. Each category will have a slightly different calculation for labor burden. For illustration purposes, imagine a contracting company that works 52 weeks per year, has six field laborers, one office worker, and an owner who handles sales, design, and general administration of the business. The charts that follows reflect this imaginary company, K&K Contractors LLC. However, the concepts work well with companies of all sizes and configurations.

When compiling the information needed to complete the calculations, some projections will have to be made. You can never truly know the future, but you can make rational estimates.

Take a look at the Figure 6–1: Labor Burden Calculation for Field Labor on page 61. At the top of the chart, total annual regular wages are listed for six employees. The totals are based on a year of 50 working weeks of 40 hours each. The remaining two weeks of the year are reserved for vacation time. Our hypothetical company, K&K Contracting LLC, has a total yearly field payroll of $187,500.

The bottom portion of the chart lists the various taxes and benefits. These are costs that relate directly to the wages of the contracting employees who work at job sites. Office personnel, sales staff, and executives are not included (unless the latter work regularly with the work crews at the job sites). Every contracting company will have a slight variation from this chart; every state has its own rates for unemployment and worker's compensation, and general liability. The various taxes and benefits of K&K Contracting are:

- *Social security and Medicare taxes.* Employers and employees each pay, in equal amounts, these taxes. The employer's portion for social security is 6.2 percent of an employee's wage, up to an annual limit set by the federal government. For 2006, the wage limit was $94,200, meaning that the maximum amount an employer must pay for one employee is $5,840.40. There is no maximum wage limit for Medicare taxes, which have a rate of 1.45 percent for the employer. Employees pay the same amounts, which are deducted from their paychecks and sent to the government by the employer.

- *State unemployment tax.* The tax rates are established by individual states and vary widely. Taxes are usually paid by the employer and not deducted from an employee's paycheck. Most states have a range of rates, so employers who lay-off more employees incur a higher tax rate. Again, most states have a taxable wage limit; after an employee's annual wage exceeds a certain amount, unemployment taxes are no longer charged to the employer. A few states offer an exemption to certain owners of the business; however, care must be taken with this option as it may result in higher federal unemployment taxes.

Figure 6–1: Labor Burden Calculation for Field Labor

Total Field Payroll	Hours Work per Year	Wage Rate	Annual Wage	Explanation of Calculation
3 Foremen	2,000 each, 6,000 total	$18.75	$112,500	$18.75 x 6,000
3 Laborers	2,000 each, 6,000 total	$12.50	$75,000	$12.50 x 6,000
Total annual wage			$187,500	

Labor Burden	Calculation Parameters	Rate	Cost	Explanation of Calculation
Social security/Medicare	percentage of total payroll	7.65%	$14,344	.0765 x $187,500
State unemployment	first $10,000 each employee	5.00%	$3,000	(.05 x $10,000) x 6 employees
Federal unemployment	first $7,000 each employee	0.80%	$336	(.008 x $7,000) x 6 employees
Worker's compensation	percentage of total payroll	9.00%	$16,875	.09 x $187,500
General liability	percentage of total payroll	1.00%	$1,875	.01 x $187,500
Paid vacations	3 foremen @ 2 weeks each		$4,500	$18.75 x 80 hours x 3 foremen
	3 laborers @ 2 weeks each		$3,000	$12.50 x 80 hours x 3 laborers
Paid holidays	7 days for 3 foremen		$3,150	$18.75 x 56 hours x 3 fopremen
	7 days for 3 laborers		$2,100	$12.50 x 56 hours x 3 laborers
Health insurance	$150 per month per employee		$7,560	$150 x 6 employees x 12 months x 70% employer contribution
	Employer pays 70%			
Overtime	time-and-a-half over 40 hours		$13,500	$18.75 x 1.5 x 4 hrs x 40 weeks x 3 foremen
	per week; estimate 4 hours		$9,000	$12.50 x 1.5 x 4 hrs x 40 weeks x 3 laborers
	per week for 40 weeks per employee			
Total Labor Burden			**$79,240**	
	Percent of total annual wage		**42.3%**	

- *Federal unemployment tax.* This tax is very simple and straightforward; employers pay 0.8 percent of the first $7,000 of each employee's wage.

- *Worker's compensation.* Once again each state has its own laws governing worker's compensation insurance, which provides coverage for employees who are injured on the job. While the states set the rates, usually in dollars per $100 of payroll, insurance companies sell the product. These insurance companies are in competition and can offer to pay a dividend (return of premium) to companies who have excellent safety records. Rates in contracting and construction are typically very high due to the risk of injury on job sites. However, dividend payments can be as much as 50 percent of the annual premium.

- *General liability.* The premiums for this insurance are based on payroll and vary from state to state and from contractor to contractor. The insurance covers several items, but the two most important features insure against damage to a client's property and against injury or harm done after a project is completed. For example, if an employee backs a vehicle into a client's garage, the general liability insurance will cover the damage; or if someone trips on a step installed by a contractor, general liability insurance will provide some protection against lawsuits and should pay for repair.

- *Paid vacations and holidays.* While these are actually employee fringe benefits, they are expected by most employees. Employers who do not offer these benefits risk losing employees to competing businesses.

- *Health insurance premiums.* Health insurance is a hot button issue these days and is often the single largest annual expense for a small business. The health insurance industry is very complex and in a constant state of change. Therefore, contractors should consult with independent insurance agents who specialize in the field. This is certainly an area where one size does not fit all. Insurance agents can shop around to find the best plan for each contracting company. Typically, employers ask each employee to contribute a portion of the premiums.

- *Overtime.* Unless a contractor can charge its clients extra when an employee works more than 40 hours per week, the cost of overtime should be included in the labor burden. In the case of K&K Contracting, each worker is estimated to work 44 hours a week for 40 weeks and 40 hours for the remaining 12 weeks of the year. The federal government has ruled that in general employers must pay a wage of one and one-half time a worker's regular wage for each hour over 40 worked in one week.

Beware!
Some employees must be paid overtime even if they are paid a salary. The rules are complex, so make sure you understand which of your employees must receive time-and-a-half when they work more than 40 hours in a week.

As we see on Figure 6–1, the total labor burden for K&K Contracting LLC is just over $79,000 per year for its six employees. Therefore, the annual labor costs are far higher than the regular wages paid to employees. But how is this information useful to the budget and estimating process? Simple, really. You calculate the labor burden's cost as a percentage of total field payroll by dividing the labor burden by the total payroll as follows:

$$\$79,239 \div \$187,500 = .423 = 42.3\%$$

This means that if you pay an employee $10 per hour, your true cost is $14.23 per hour. You determine this by multiplying $10 by .423, which equals $4.23, and then adding the two numbers. This is a very useful method because if you hire an additional laborer during the course of the year, the extra costs of carrying that employee on your payroll (the labor burden) will be automatically included in your budget.

As indicated earlier, labor costs are only one part of direct costs; the remainder includes estimated annual costs for materials, equipment rental, and subcontractors. In Figure 6–2, I've set up a hypothetical direct cost budget for K&K Contracting.

Figure 6–2: Direct Cost Budget

Direct Costs Budget for 2xxx

	Annual Expense
ABC Contractors Supply	$85,000.00
Continental Materials	$110,000.00
USA Hardware	$35,000.00
County Builders & Supply	$55,000.00
Jones & Jones Lumber	$30,000.00
All-State-Rent-It-All	$17,500.00
National Plastics	$25,000.00
Foremans' wages	$101,250.00
Laborers' wages	$67,500.00
Labor burden @ 42.3%	$71,381.25
Total Direct Costs	**$597,631.25**

Astute readers will notice that the cost of labor listed in the direct cost budget, given in Figure 6–2, ($101,250 + $67,500 = $168,750) does not equal the total annual wage ($187,500) listed on the labor burden worksheet, Figure 6–1. The reason for this is that I am reserving 10 percent of the cost of labor for what is called "yard time," which is the cost of paying employees when they are not on the job sites generating revenues. They may be maintaining equipment, taking part in staff meetings, attending job related seminars, on break, or performing warranty work. Every company will have its own calculation for yard time. But for the purposes of this book, I'll use 10 percent (about four hours per week, average, per employee).

Therefore, K&K Contractors expects to spend approximately $600,000 for materials and labor that are used expressly for the projects it works on. I'll save this amount for now and come back to its after I set a budget for the other two categories of spending.

Fixed Costs

Every business has costs that it incurs regardless of the level of business activity. These are amounts due on a regular basis and are fairly constant from one year to the next when adjusted for inflation. Fixed costs include expenditures for items such as:

- Officer and office salaries
- Interest expense
- Rent and utilities
- Telephone service
- Some advertising

For example, a company pays a fixed amount of rent each month for its office space regardless of how busy it might be; it signs a lease agreement for $1,000 per month and must pay that amount whether its annual revenues are $100,000 or $2,000,000. However, some fixed costs may "break the rule" and increase more than an increase in revenues. Telephone service is one example: if revenues unexpectedly surge, a company may have to add additional telephone lines to handle the increased business. But for the purposes of this book, assume that fixed costs will remain relatively constant. However, before the fixed cost budget category is set up, the labor burden for the office staff must be determined. Refer to Figure 6–3 on page 65, which is very similar to Figure 6–1.

You can make the same mathematical calculation used in Figure 6–1 to determine the labor burden as a percentage of total office payroll as shown:

$$\$14,769 \div \$75,000 = .197 \text{ or } 19.7\%$$

This is much lower than the labor burden for field labor, primarily because worker's compensation rates are much lower for office workers and because holidays, vacations, and overtime are included in the salaries of these workers. Once again, for every $10 that you pay office staff, you'll pay an additional $1.97 to the various state

Figure 6–3: Office Staff Labor Burden

Office Payroll	Hours Work per Year	Wage Rate	Annual Wage	Explanation of Calculation
Owner	salary	$50,000	$50,000	
Assistant	salary	$25,000	$25,000	
Total annual wage			**$75,000**	

Labor Burden	Calculation Parameters	Rate	Cost	Explanation of Calculation
Social security/Medicare	percentage of total payroll	7.65%	$5,737.50	.0765 x $75,000
State unemployment	first $10,000 each employee	5.00%	$1,000	(.05 x $10,000) x 2 employees
Federal unemployment	first $7,000 each employee	0.80%	$112	(.008 x $7,000) x 2 employees
Worker's compensation	percentage of total payroll	2.00%	$1,500	.02 x $75,000
General liability	percentage of total payroll	1.00%	$750	.01 x $75,000
Paid vacations	Included in salary		$0	
Paid holidays	Included in salary		$0	
Health insurance	Employer pays 70%		$5,670	Owner: $500 per month, assistant: $175 per month
Overtime	None		$0	
Total Labor Burden			**$14,770**	
	Percent of total annual wage		19.7%	

Figure 6–4: Fixed Cost Budget

Fixed Costs Budget for 2xxx

	Annual Expense
Kate's salary	$40,000
Ken's salary	$40,000
Office assistant salary	$24,000
Labor burden @ 19.7%	$20,488
Insurance (building/vehicle)	$3,000
Health insurance (office staff)	$10,000
Telephone	$900
Cellular phones (5)	$3,000
Yellow Pages advertising	$1,200
Bank payments	$25,000
Capital equipment fund	$5,000
Licenses	$1,200
Utilities	$1,800
Rent	$12,000
Total Fixed Costs	**$187,588**

and federal governments and for fringe benefits. Putting together the fixed cost budget results in Figure 6–4, above.

Several items in the fixed cost budget need further explanation and clarification.

- *Health insurance*. As previously noted, the company pays for 70 percent of the premium while each employee contributes the remaining 30 percent.

- *Bank payments*. I include both principal and interest paid for the bank loans secured to buy equipment. Since the budget is concerned with actual spending, I'll leave income tax ramifications to the accountant. Interest payments are a deductible expense and therefore can help reduce income taxes; principal payments are not deductible in the same way as interest payments. However, equipment purchases can be depreciated over time, reducing the income tax burden. Depreciation can be a complex concept; I strongly recommend consulting with an accountant in order to receive the most favorable benefit from depreciating equipment.

- *Capital equipment fund.* While this is an optional expense, I strongly recommend establishing a fund to be used to purchase equipment or to make a down payment on a loan for equipment. Companies with very good credit ratings can often secure bank loans for the total purchase price of a piece of equipment. However, by creating a separate capital equipment fund, future principal and interest payments can be reduced, thereby improving the monthly cash flow of the business. An excellent way to plan for the future is to prepare a chart listing all of your depreciable equipment, such as vehicles and skid loaders, and projecting the useful life of each. Then estimate the replacement cost, adjusting for inflation. Knowing when and how much you will have to borrow for capital equipment is critical to both the current and future annual budget process. Saving for the future takes good planning and great discipline, but is well worth the time and effort.

- *Other items.* The fixed-cost budget is fairly simple, but realistic for a small business. Some other expenses that companies include in their fixed-cost budget are: employer portion of retirement plans, professional expenses such as attendance at trade shows or seminars, internet web hosting costs, association dues, and other employee fringe benefits.

- *Anticipate.* When compiling the information for your fixed-cost budget, remember to include items that may increase later in the year due to other spending. For example, if you plan to purchase a new vehicle in September, remember to add the cost of insurance for the last four months of the year as well as the cost of the license plate.

Dollar Stretcher

Log on the internet and go to www.bankrate.com. Here you'll be able to find a list of financial institutions that offer the most competitive money market and savings accounts. Bankrate.com also gives each institution "Safe & Sound," rating which assesses the financial condition of the banks, thrifts, and credit unions.

To review, the fixed-cost budget for K&K Contracting amounts to $175,588, meaning that the company expects to spend that much regardless of the amount of revenues that are generated during the year. It is crucial that the fixed-cost budget be realistic and accurate because it not only impacts the pricing of services, it also helps determine the annual revenue required to make a profit. I'll come back to the profit issue later in this chapter.

Variable Costs

The third category of spending is called variable expenses because items here usually change in real terms, or dollar amounts, as the level of business activity increases. In addition, they tend to remain about the same *percentage* of direct costs. In other words, if direct costs increase from one year to the next by 15 percent, it is likely that as a group variable costs will also rise approximately 15 percent. An example of variable costs is the cost of postage. When business activity increases, a company is likely to send more mail (in spite of increase in the use of e-mail, fax machines, and online banking), both to pay more supplier invoices and to send more proposals, invoices, and general correspondence to clients. Other types of expenses that I include in variable costs are:

- Vehicle maintenance and repairs
- Gas, diesel fuel, oil
- Office expenses
- Printing
- Employee incentive or bonus pay
- Some advertising
- Small tools; hardware
- Uniforms
- Salesperson salaries and commissions

Some costs overlap between fixed and variable. These include items such as advertising and cellular phone service. While the cost of advertising in the Yellow Pages is constant from one month to the next, advertisements in local newspapers or magazines may be placed at irregular intervals—or not at all. The cost of cell phone service is typically based on the number of minutes used per month; however, as business activity increases, employees may exceed the limits set by their cellular phone provider or additional phones may be needed for new employees, thereby increasing monthly costs.

The variable cost budget for K&K Contracting given in Figure 6–5 on page 69 is fairly easy to understand. These are the costs that will change as business activity changes. I strongly recommend including a budget for

Beware!
In most states, price fixing of a product or service is illegal. Generally speaking, a company may not, with another company, agree to set a price for a particular product or service. However, conformity of prices for a particular product or service is not illegal unless the conformity was created in combination with other companies agreeing on a set price.

Figure 6–5: Variable Cost Budget

Variable Cost Budget for 2xxx

Miscellaneous expenses	$6,000	
Gasoline/diesel fuel	$15,000	
Advertising	$5,000	special sales, magazine ads, fliers
Postage	$750	
Printing	$1,000	invoice forms, blank checks, contract forms
Office supplies	$4,000	envelopes, computer supplies
Hardware store/small tools	$3,000	upkeep of property;
Equipment repairs	$10,000	vehicles and equipment
Uniforms	$900	
Employee yard time	$18,750	estimated at 10% of wage cost
Employee incentives and bonuses	$6,000	employee awards
Labor burden @ 42.3%	$10,469	
Cell phones (portion)	$300	
Contingency	$2,000	
Returns	$3,000	warranty work
Total Variable Costs	**$86,169**	

"contingency." Unfortunately, you can expect the unexpected—as when the United States experienced a jump in the price of gasoline to well over $3 per gallon. Employee incentives are in the variable cost budget even though they may not increase as revenues increase. However, they are certainly not fixed costs, and it would be a stretch to include them in direct costs. Because they are usually tied to employee performance, the best place for them is with variable costs.

Overhead

When a company has been in operation for two or three years, it's much easier to pull these numbers together and create a reasonable budget that includes direct costs, fixed costs, and variable costs. For newer companies without a track record, the task is much more difficult. Some guesswork may be needed. Still, consulting with others in your industry can usually be beneficial. The purpose of any consultation is not to set prices, but to learn general concepts and broad ranges of cost relationships. One should never be afraid to ask for help or guidance; the worst that can happen is someone says no.

Well, now what? Direct costs, fixed costs, and variable costs are identified as the major components of a budget. This is all well and good, but what does it tell you and how can you benefit from the knowledge gained from compiling these budget numbers? First it's a valuable exercise that forces a business owner to correctly identify all of the costs of doing business. But more importantly, you can use the information to assist in setting prices for your products and services.

Now that you've identified three categories of spending, the next step is to combine two of them and give them a new name. Each will keep its own identity, but they work together to make what is called "overhead." Overhead is the ongoing general and administrative expenses that are not directly related to the selling of a company's goods and services. To that end, you'll combine fixed costs and variable costs to calculate total overhead expense. Using the example of K&K Contracting, combining these costs gives the following results:

$$\text{Fixed costs} = \$187,588$$
$$\underline{+ \text{ Variable costs} = \$ \ 86,169}$$
$$= \text{Overhead} = \$273,757$$

One way to consider overhead is that it supports direct costs. When money is spent specifically to generate revenues (direct costs), money is also spent in the office and elsewhere to support those direct costs. The budget you are developing will help you determine how you will generate revenues to pay for or to *recover* overhead expenses. The first step is to understand the relationship between direct costs and overhead. Consider this formula:

Total overhead ÷ Direct costs = Overhead recovery percent

And when we plug in our numbers:

$\$273,757 \div \$597,631 = .458$ or 46% = Overhead

What this means is that for every $100 spent on direct costs an additional $46 will be spent on overhead. With a little experience, it is fairly easy to determine the cost of materials for a project as well as the time estimated to complete it. Once this is accomplished, the cost of overhead recovery falls right into place.

Alternative Method

Some contractors, either by preference or because the competition demands it, allocate overhead only to their labor costs. In the case of K&K Contracting, when overhead is allocated to labor only, the overhead recovery rate is 114 percent ($273,575 ÷ $ 240,131).This may be acceptable for some companies, especially if the relationship between materials and labor is relatively constant. However, when the cost of materials is extremely high relative to the cost of labor, the result is usually to undercharge the client. The reverse is usually true when the cost of labor is high relative to the cost of materials.

In Figure 6–6 on page 72, the costs of four separate projects are presented using two different methods. Method A allocates overhead evenly between materials and labor, while Method B allocates overhead to labor costs only. As can be seen by the results, Method B shows no constant relationship to Method A: differences range from +45 percent to –7 percent. Regardless of the inconsistencies, I recommend testing these methods both internally and against the competition to determine if one of the methods is preferable to the other. In fact, different divisions within one company might use different methods. A key factor is to remain competitive with the other contractors in your area while making a reasonable profit.

Break-Even Point

Break-even revenue is achieved when your product or service stops costing you money to produce and sell and begins to generate a profit. Refer to Figure 6–6 and study the data for Project A. Method A, numbers I will use for the remainder of this book, which indicates a break-even point of $722. This includes the wage costs and associated labor burden to complete the project as well as all of the overhead related to these direct costs. As long as the costs stay within this budget, the company will begin to make a profit when they receive more than $722 for the project.

Budget Overview

Let's summarize the annual budget by combining the information gathered in Figures 6–2, 6–4, and 6–5. These include all of the anticipated costs of doing business during the entire year. In the next section, I break out the numbers and show how to prepare an estimate for an individual project. Following is the summary of the charts:

Figure 6–6: Comparison of Overhead Recovery Methods

	Project A	Project B	Project C	Project D
Cost of materials	$50	$50	$5,000	$5,000
Hours to do the job	20	100	20	100
Wage cost @ $15.625 per hour	$313	$1,563	$313	$1,563
Labor burden @ .423	$132	$661	$132	$661
Wage cost + labor burden	$445	$2,223	$445	$2,223
Method A: Allocate overhead equally to materials and labor				
Materials + labor	$495	$2,273	$5,445	$7,223
Overhead @ 46%	$228	$1,046	$2,505	$3,323
Break-even point	$722	$3,319	$7,949	$10,546
Method B: Allocate overhead to cost of labor only				
Cost of materials	$50	$50	$5,000	$5,000
Wage cost + labor burden	$445	$2,223	$445	$2,223
Overhead @ 114% (of labor only)	$507	$2,535	$507	$2,535
Break-even point	$1,002	$4,808	$5,952	$9,758
Effect	**Difference**	**Difference**	**Difference**	**Difference**
	+39%	**+45%**	**−25%**	**−7%**

Direct costs   = $ 597,631
Fixed costs   = $ 187,588 = 31.4% of Direct costs
Variable costs = $ 86,169 = 14.4% of Direct costs
Total costs   = $871,388

Fixed costs and variable costs are the components of overhead because they are the expenses that support the direct costs, the expenses directly related to the implementation of projects. As indicated earlier, total overhead in this case is 46 percent of direct costs. At this point, the level of total costs is useful only to give a general indication of how much revenue will be required to break even. However, this is true only at the level of direct costs indicated in Figure 6–2. Chapter 7 covers the concept of contribution margin and the revenues required to generate a profit.

Preparing the Estimate

Preparing an estimate for an individual client can be a relatively easy task once an annual budget has been set and the cost of materials for the project determined. The only other major piece of information required is the amount of labor required to complete the project. The best way to do this is to make a chart of all the individual tasks your company does and assign a time budget for each. Each task should indicate the units involved (each, square feet, cubic yards, etc.) and the time required for a single employee to complete the task. Refer to Figure 6–7 below for an example from a hypothetical landscape contracting company:

With this information in hand, you can begin to develop an estimate. I'll go through the process step-by-step using the following information. Upon completion, I'll use a spreadsheet to calculate a price for the job.

Figure 6–7: Time Required per Task

Task	Unit	Time
Prepare plant bed	square foot	.025 hours
Plant 36" shrub	each	0.40 hours
Plant 2" shade trees	each	2.5 hours
Mulch plant beds	cubic yard	.75 hours
Stake trees	each	.30 hours
Install drain tile	linear foot	.50 hours
Spread topsoil	cubic yard	.35 hours
Sow grass seed	pound	.15 hours

- Calculate average crew wage
- Compile list of materials needed for the project
- Refer to the time-per-task chart
- Find the labor burden and overhead recovery percentages
- Decide the desired profit

Figure 6–8 on page 75 demonstrates a simple estimate using the spreadsheet:

- Column A is a list of the materials and tasks planned for the job.
- Column B indicates the unit associated with Column A.
- Column C shows the total quantity of each unit.
- Column D is the individual cost of each item.
- Column E is the total material cost achieved by multiplying column C by column D.
- Column F indicates the time it takes for one worker to complete one task; see Figure 6–7.
- Column G shows the total time to complete all tasks; Column F times Column C.
- Row 9 shows the totals of both the materials and the time required to complete the project.
- Row 11 indicates the average crew wage (see below).
- Row 12 indicates the total wage cost, including the labor burden calculated in Figure 6–1.
- Row 13 is the total direct cost for the project.
- Row 15 is the cost of overhead from page 86.
- Row 16 is the sum of Row 18 and Row 20, showing the break-even point of the project.

The average crew wage needs a bit more explanation. Step 1 is to add the wages of the individual workers expected to work on the project and divide by the number of workers; Step 2 adds the labor burden. The concept is to find an average crew wage because this ties in directly with the information from Figure 6–7. An average crew wage is the *average paid to one worker* while the time required per task is the amount of *time required for one worker* to complete the task. If K&K Contracting decides to place one two-person crew on the project, the wages of the two workers are $18.75 and $12.50:

Step 1: ($18.75 + $12.50) ÷ 2 = $15.625 per hour = average crew wage

Step 2: $15.625 x labor burden percent from Figure 6–1
$15.625 x .423 = $6.61 = average labor burden per employee
$15.625 + $6.61 = $22.24 per hour = average crew wage

Figure 6–8: Simple Estimate

	A	B	C	D	E	F	G	H
	Description	Unit	Quantity	Unit Cost of Material	Total Cost of Materials	Time per Task Notes	Total Time in Hours	Explanation
1	Prepare plant bed	sq. feet	200	$0	$0	0.03	5.00	
2	2" shade trees	each	2	$100	$200	2.50	5.00	
3	36" shrub	each	5	$35	$175	0.40	2.00	
4	Stake trees	each	2	$5	$10	0.30	0.60	
5	Mulch	Cubic yard	3	$20	$60	0.75	2.25	
6	Spread topsoil	cubic yard	20	$20	$400	0.35	7.00	
7	Sow grass seed	pound	5	$4	$20	0.15	0.75	
8								
9	Totals				$865		22.60	
10								
11	Average crew wage						$22.24	
12	Cost of labor						$502.62	22.60 hours x $22.24
13	Total direct cost						$1,367.62	Materials plus labor
14	Overhead recovery %						46%	
15	Overhead cost						$629.11	$1367.62 x 0.46
16	Break-even point						$1,996.73	$1367.72 + $629.11

Therefore, we entered $22.24 in Row 15 of the spreadsheet and used the time per task information to calculate the total cost of labor for the project (Row 16).

The method used in this example is very beneficial because it can be used even if the number of workers on the project changes. Using the spreadsheet, it was determined that it will take one worker 22.60 actual hours to complete the project; with two workers the project should be completed in 11.30 actual hours. Should the owners decide to add another two-person work crew, they'd be free to do so without worrying about the effect on the bottom line.

Profits: The Bottom Line

"The worst crime against the working people is a company which fails to operate at a profit."

—SAMUEL GOMPERS, WHO FOUNDED
THE AMERICAN FEDERATION OF LABOR IN 1886

Thus far I've discussed only the cost of doing business, without regard to revenues or profits. You've learned that there are costs that are directly related to the process of implementing a project; then there are overhead costs, some of which are related to the direct costs and others that will be incurred regardless of the amount of direct costs. Profit is what you have left over after paying all your expenses. If you were to study the income statement of a large corporation like the Walt Disney Company, you'd find columns and rows with data showing "gross profit," "operating income," "income before tax," "income after tax," "income before extraordinary items," and "net income." The discussion of these items is left to the accounting professors. The focus here is on net income.

Stat Fact

According to industry sources, the average net income as a percentage of revenues within the contracting industry ranges from 3 to 5 percent. This means that a company with $1 million in revenues can expect to have a net income, after all expenses, of between $30,000 and $50,000.

However, net income is not the only measure of financial success. Investment advisors and specialists consider many factors when studying the financial statements of corporations. Again, it can be a very complex and time-consuming process to understand the profitability and success of a business. For my purposes here, I'll keep it simple. While every owner must determine what level of profit is acceptable, I'll use 12 percent as a profit goal when pricing services. Using this as a benchmark will allow for payment of year-end

Accounting 101

Accountants, financial officers, and investors study financial statements in many different ways. I'll touch on three terms that sound similar but are quite different. While there are no "magic numbers," it may be an interesting and useful exercise to track these ratios on an annual basis. If the ratios increase, you can smile; if they decrease, don't frown, just work harder and more efficiently.

1. Return on Equity equals net profit after taxes divided by stockholders' equity. It measures a company's efficiency at generating profits from dollars invested in the business. Return on Equity is irrelevant if earnings are not reinvested in the company.

2. Return on Assets equals net profit after taxes divided by total assets. It's an important gauge of profitability as it gives insight into the ability of management to generate profits from the assets available to the company.

3. Return on Capital equals net income after taxes divided by long term debt plus common stock. It is a measure of how effectively a company uses the money, both borrowed and owned, that is invested in the company.

bonuses or dividends, upgrade buildings and equipment, and build up an emergency fund.

The question is how to determine the price to charge and make a 12 percent profit. If you refer to Figure 6–8 we see that the break-even point for the project is $1,997. Many people would venture a guess and say "to make a 12 percent profit, just multiply $1,997 by 12 percent and add the two numbers." Well, they are wrong. If you just read this sentence and shook your head, you are not alone. Now read the next sentence carefully and memorize it:

To make a 12 percent profit on a project, divide the break-even point by one minus the desired profit (shown as a decimal).

Read it again. To make a 12 percent profit, you divide the break-even point by 0.88.

An example will make this seemingly crazy mathematical formula make sense. Suppose you sell a product for $100 and make a 10 percent profit; your break-even point is $100 – $10, or $90. However, if you add 10 percent to $90, you get $99, $1 short of what you want. However, if you divide $90 by (1.00 – .10), you arrive back at $100.

Now go back to Figure 6–8 with a break-even point of $1,997. To charge enough to make a 12 percent profit, you divide $1,997 by 0.88 and come up with a final cost of $2269.

Chapter 6 Highlights

★ Many new businesses fail because they fail to properly manage their finances.

★ Establishing a financial budget is a key ingredient to business success.

★ Computer spreadsheets are invaluable tools for establishing a budget.

★ The true cost of labor includes payroll taxes, government mandated insurance, employee benefits, and overtime.

★ Overhead is comprised of fixed costs and variable costs.

★ Pricing systems must be designed to recover overhead expenses.

★ Three elements determine the final price to the consumer: direct labor and materials costs, overhead recovery, and profit.

★ Profits are not made until revenues reach the break-even point.

Contribution Margin
The Key to
Understanding Profits

For those of you who are still scratching your heads over the Accounting 101 sidebar in the last chapter, rest easy. You are not alone. The fact of the matter is that math scares lots of people, primarily because the language of math is so different from normal human communication. For fun, take the little quiz in the Math Worksheet below to test your potential for math prowess.

> *"Mathematics is made up of 50 percent formulas, 50 percent proofs, and 50 percent imagination."*
>
> —Unknown

How many were you able to check off? For those of you who know all ten terms, you are in the wrong field. Close the book and contact M.I.T. immediately. But seriously, knowledge of higher math is not a requirement for success in business. Even those with limited exposure to algebra should be able to master the concepts of contribution margin presented in this chapter. The major difficulty is initially estimating the amount of annual revenues your company expects to generate. Once again, I suggest communicating with industry associations, fellow contractors, and former employers to arrive at a reasonable revenue projection.

How to Calculate Contribution Margin

Contribution margin is a valuable mathematical tool that will help with your financial planning in two important ways. First, it will tell you how much revenue you must

---

Math Worksheet

Study the following ten math terms. Place a check mark next to the ones you understand or can define. (No cheating allowed!)

___ Algorithm

___ Exponential Function

___ Divergence theorem

___ Permutations

___ Heaviside function

___ Differential equation

___ Distributive property

___ Transitive property

___ Scientific number

___ Sigma notation

generate during the year in order to break even, and second, how much profit you will make on each dollar of revenue after reaching your break-even point.

Contribution margin is defined as "the amount of revenue remaining after paying direct costs and variable costs that is available to pay fixed costs and profits." It is used as both a dollar amount and as a percentage.

The formula I will use for contribution margin is:

Contribution margin (CM) =
Revenues – (Direct costs + Variable costs)

Using the example in Chapter 6 on page 70, and taking a bit of artistic license and estimating annual revenues at $900,000, you arrive at the following contribution margin:

Beware!

"Profit" as used in this book is unlike the actual taxable profit that a company reports on its state and federal income tax forms. Other factors, such as depreciation and prepaid expenses, have an effect on taxes due. In addition, the accounting method, cash or accrual, has significant effect on taxes. This is just another reason why it is critical to engage a qualified accountant to plan year-end tax strategy and to prepare tax returns.

$$CM = \$900,000 - (\$597,631 + \$86,169)$$
$$CM = \$900,000 - \$683,800$$
$$CM = \$216,200$$

What this shows is that you have $216,200 available to pay for fixed costs, the expenses that do not change even when revenue changes, and profit.

A new formula calculates the contribution margin *ratio*:

Contribution margin ratio (CMR) = Contribution margin ÷ revenues

$$CMR = \$216,200 \div \$900,000$$
$$CMR = 0.2402 \text{ (or } 24.02\%)$$

For accuracy, I recommend carrying out the fraction to four decimal points. For you math cowards, I am nearly finished with formulas. If you read this chapter several times and work through the calculations yourself, it will become much clearer to you. You might even try the formulas with different estimated revenue figures to learn the effect on your budget.

The contribution margin ratio has two useful functions. First, you'll determine, based on fixed costs, at what point your revenue produces a break-even situation. The contribution margin ratio will probably change from year to year, and I recommend tracking the ratio and using a two- or three-year average when you set up your annual budget. Here's another useful formula:

$$\text{Break-even point (BEP)} = \text{Fixed costs} \div \text{CMR}$$
$$\text{BEP} = \$187,588 \div 0.2402$$
$$\text{BEP} = \$780,965$$

This means that if actual fixed costs meet the budget, the company will begin to generate a profit when revenues exceed \$780,965. How much of a profit will be made is revealed by using the following (and final) formula:

$$\text{Profit} = (\text{Revenue} - \text{Break-even revenue}) \times \text{CMR}$$
$$\text{Profit} = (\$900,000 - \$780,965) \times 0.2402$$
$$\text{Profit} = \$119,035 \times 0.2402$$
$$\text{Profit} = \$28,592$$

Even though actual revenue exceeds break-even revenue by more than \$119,000, the actual profit is far less because the difference was used for direct and variable costs spent generating the additional income.

For most contracting businesses, the ideal time to reach the break-even point is in early fall; doing so leaves several months to generate a profit. If the break-even point is reached in December, for example, the profit will likely be small. Study Figure 7–1, and it should become clear.

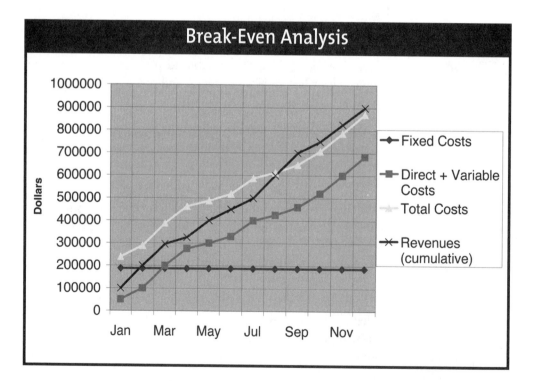

Figure 7–1 shows how revenues and expenses grow during the year. Total costs, which include direct, fixed, and variable costs, are shown by the line with arrows. Revenues are shown by the line with tiny x's. In the example, revenues begin to exceed costs during the month of August and remain ahead of costs for the remainder of the year, resulting in a profit for the company.

The Doctor Is In

Establishing a budget, understanding and using contribution margin, and correctly allocating expenses among direct, fixed, and variable costs are only the first step in implementing a successful budget and estimating system. In order to be successful, expenses and revenues must be monitored on a regular basis, and adjusted if necessary. The budget should be reviewed at least monthly for most small contracting businesses and at least quarterly for larger companies. A budget is not a static document, but is subject to change and modification during the year. A change in the budget may necessitate a change in the way products and services are estimated, resulting in a price change. The sooner that a company can determine that expenses are not meeting budget expectations, the sooner pricing can be adjusted to reflect the discrepancies.

Figure 7–2 on page 84 is an example of monitoring spending on a monthly basis. Spending through September is compared with the 12-month budget. Column 2 lists the amounts, by category that are budgeted for the entire year; column 3 lists the amounts actually spent as of September 30; column 4 indicates the percentage of the annual budget that has been spent. Because September represents 75 percent of the year, the expectation is that most expense categories be close to this figure. Amounts that are far over or far under the budget should be analyzed further.

While several items are over budget, as shown in bold type, the totals for each category are acceptable; total direct costs are 76 percent of budget, fixed costs are right on budget at 75 percent, and variable costs are under budget at 68 percent. Two items are worth considering in more detail. Utilities have an annual budget of $1,800, but $1,550, or 86 percent of budget has been spent. An analysis may show that seasonal temperatures caused utility expenses to rise earlier in the year, but they are expected to drop in later months. The uniforms expenses are at 100 percent of budget. Here, an analysis may indicate that new uniforms were purchased in January. No more uniforms will be purchased before the end of the year, so the annual expense will meet the budget. In the example of Figure 7–2, it appears that total spending is very close to the budget and there is no need to adjust the pricing formula.

A second method of tracking the success or failure of company operations has little to do with the budget or with contribution margin. However, it is a useful tool, especially when used over the course of several years. This method compares actual

Figure 7–2: Get a Checkup

Direct Cost Budget		Spent through 9/30/xx	
	Annual Expense	75% of the Year	Percent of Total Budget Spent
ABC Contractors Supply	$85,000	$65,000	76%
Continental Materials	$110,000	$80,000	73%
USA Hardware	$35,000	$32,000	**91%**
County Builders & Supply	$55,000	$42,500	77%
Jones & Jones Lumber	$30,000	$24,000	**80%**
All-State-Rent-It-All	$17,500	$10,000	57%
National Plastics	$25,000	$15,000	60%
Foremans' wages	$101,250	$80,000	**79%**
Laborers' wages	$67,500	$52,000	77%
Labor burden @ 42.3%	$71,381	$55,836	78%
Total direct costs	$597,631	$456,336	76%

Fixed Cost Budget			
Kate's salary	$40,000	$30,000	75%
Ken's salary	$40,000	$30,000	75%
Office assistant salary	$24,000	$18,000	75%
Labor burden @ 19.7%	$20,488	$15,366	75%
Insurance (building/vehicle)	$3,000	$2,300	77%
Health insurance (office staff)	$10,000	$7,500	75%
Telephone	$900	$700	78%
Cellular phones (5)	$3,000	$2,500	**83%**
Yellow pages advertising	$1,200	$900	75%
Bank payments	$25,000	$18,750	75%
Capital equipment fund	$5,000	$3,750	75%

Figure 7–2: Get a Checkup, continued

	Annual Expense	75% of the Year	Percent of Total Budget Spent
Fixed Cost Budget, continued			
Licenses	$1,200	$900	75%
Utilities	$1,800	$1,550	**86%**
Rent	$12,000	$9,000	75%
Total Fixed Costs	$187,588	$141,216	75%
% of Direct Costs	31%	31%	
Variable Cost Budget			
Miscellaneous expenses	$6,000	$4,000	67%
Gasoline/diesel fuel	$15,000	$13,000	**87%**
Advertising	$5,000	$4,000	**80%**
Postage	$750	$500	67%
Printing	$1,000	$500	50%
Office supplies	$4,000	$3,000	75%
Hardware store/small tools	$3,000	$2,450	**82%**
Equipment repairs	$10,000	$4,000	40%
Uniforms	$900	$900	**100%**
Employee yard time	$18,750	$13,500	72%
Employee incentives & bonuses	$6,000	$3,500	58%
Labor burden @ 42.3%	$10,469	$7,191	69%
Cell phones (portion)	$300	$250	**83%**
Contingency	$2,000	$100	5%
Returns	$3,000	$2,000	67%
Total Variable Costs	$86,169	$58,891	68%
% of Direct Costs	14%	13%	

Figure 7–3: Sales per Labor Dollar

Year	Month	Revenues	Regular Wages	Overtime	Total Wages	Sales per Labor Dollar
2004	September	$580,000	$117,500	$10,000	$127,500	$4.55
2005	September	$625,000	$129,000	$11,500	$140,500	$4.45
2006	September	$675,000	$135,000	$12,000	$147,000	$4.59

revenues with real field labor costs, which are regular wages plus overtime costs. It is not necessary to add labor burden to the calculations. Wages of office staff, sales staff, and executives are not included as they are not direct job costs. Consider Figure 7–3.

As shown, by at the end of September 2004, revenues were $580,000 and total wages were $127,500. Therefore, each dollar spent on field wages generated $4.55 of revenue. In 2005, the amount generated dropped to $4.45, but it rebounded in 2006 to $4.59. For some reason, efficiency dropped in 2005; there could be any number of reasons for this drop, and they aren't necessarily all bad. It may be that the workforce did work less efficiently and took longer than expected to complete projects. It may also be just a quirk in the calendar—perhaps there was an extra pay period in 2005 or, possibly, several projects were near completion at the end of the month and their revenues are not factored into the equation. But whenever there is a drop in efficiency as indicated by a reduction in sales-per-labor dollar, it is necessary to learn why the drop occurred. Any drop in efficiency is a red flag that may indicate a breakdown somewhere in the company. Perhaps the estimating department did not realize that there was a price increase in materials, or new employees are taking too long to learn there tasks, or the billing department is tardy in sending invoices for work completed. Whatever the reason, it must be corrected immediately.

Tracking expenditures and revenues on a monthly basis and comparing them to the annual budget and to previous years' spending is a fairly simple task that should be done on a monthly basis, shortly after the end of each month. Routine financial checkups will usually prevent serious problems that can have a negative impact on a company's bottom line.

Chapter 7 Highlights

★ Contribution margin is defined as "the amount of revenue remaining after paying direct and variable costs that is available to pay fixed costs and for profit."

★ Contribution margin is used to calculate at what point during the year revenues produce a break-even situation.

★ Contribution margin is used to determine how much profit is made from each dollar of revenue after the break-even point is reached.

★ Small businesses should schedule a monthly "physical exam" to ensure that spending is in line with expectations.

8

Promoting Your
Services

Company logos come in all sizes, shapes, and colors. A few, like the Nike Swoosh and McDonald's Golden Arches, are so recognizable that the companies don't need to include their name with the logo. Many professional sports team simply have the Swoosh sewn onto their uniforms; viewers instantly identify the logo with Nike. Children riding in the back seat of their parent's car do not need to be told that a McDonald's is just past the next intersection; the Golden Arches (although less prominent in recent years) announce the fact well in advance. These companies have spent millions of dollars establishing worldwide images that are directly linked to their logos.

"If you don't do it excellently, don't do it at all. Because if it's not excellent, it won't be profitable or fun, and if you're not in business for fun or profit, what the hell are you doing there?"

—ROBERT TOWNSEND

Unfortunately, small contracting companies do not have the resources to develop and promote such a recognizable logo. However, this fact should not prevent them from presenting a positive image to the public.

The term "marketing" has quite a few definitions, which vary widely depending upon the type of product or service being sold. The marketing strategy for a company selling toothpaste to consumers is much different than that of a company selling steel to automobile companies. However, simply put, "marketing" is any activity that connects producers with consumers. Marketers use knowledge of economics, psychology, sociology, anthropology, and strategy to project a positive image that increases demand for their products. Most contracting companies concentrate their marketing activities on customer needs, rather than product innovation. They ask, "What do our customers need and how can we efficiently and profitably meet these needs?"

While many aspects of marketing may sound complicated and expensive, there are things that a new contracting company can do to promote itself to prospective customers without employing an expensive public relations company.

Fun Fact

Nike developed its swoosh logo in the early 1970s. Company founder Phil Knight was facing a deadline and needed a logo. He paid the handsome sum of $35 for the swoosh design, commenting that he didn't love it. He eventually gave the designer stock in the company. I bet he really loves the logo today.

Self-Promotion

One successful trick of the trade is to promote your company through the use of nonpaid coverage in local newspapers or magazines. Many newspapers have a Sunday home improvement section that offers tips and suggestions for home remodeling and landscaping. The editors of these sections are constantly looking for the local expert to assist in the development of articles. A contractor who is mentioned in the article or offers money-saving tips will gain instant credibility as an expert and reach many potential new customers at the same time. I know of a landscaping company in the Midwest that volunteered its employees to help eradicate invasive weeds at a local county park. The result was a front page article with several photographs showing the employees spraying the weeds with an herbicide. The only cost to the company was several hours of labor and a bit of chemicals; the goodwill and positive image projected by the company was invaluable. In the eyes of many consumers, this company became the local expert for control of invasive weeds. One of the goals of such an endeavor is to let the community know what the company does in a positive and constructive way. Becoming the local expert who sees a problem and offers a solution will pay dividends well beyond the cost of time spent preparing for the event.

Another approach to marketing and public relations is to offer free services to the community. Local nonprofit organizations hold fundraising events during the year and are constantly looking for items for an auction or a raffle. Contractors with design services can offer their services to help these organizations raise money. Others may donate coupons that offer savings on either products or services. Here again, the cost to the contractor is relatively small and the goodwill very large.

New companies can issue press releases to their local newspapers informing the public of these charitable endeavors. However, press releases can go further as well by announcing what's new at the company—be it new employees, employee promotions, new products and services, or company milestones.

Telling your story to a reporter or editor is not an easy task, and it may take time before writers have enough confidence in you to use your story or ask for your expert opinion. Get to know the reporter or editor personally and periodically check in with them. When they get ready to write an article, they'll remember to contact you before your competitor.

Use the Internet

Advances in technology have dramatically changed the way people communicate and the way they learn. The internet has not only transformed the lives of individuals around the world, it has changed the way most companies conduct their business.

Microsoft Corporation, a pioneer software company, formed in 1975, has a larger stock market value than 28 of the companies that comprise the Dow Jones 30 Industrial Average. (The average consists of 30 of the largest and most widely held companies in the United States.) Google, an internet search-engine company founded in 1998, has a larger market value than 19 of the Dow 30 companies. A number of these Dow 30 companies have been in business for over 100 years, yet they have less stock market value than Google and Microsoft.

This rapid growth in internet communications has been a boon for many industries around the world. Consumers have the ability to purchase nearly any product over the internet and have it delivered to their home within days. Most contracting companies do not benefit greatly from internet sales, but they can still profit by using the internet to advertise their products and services.

In recent years, a new industry that caters specifically to the internet has evolved. Web designers and web hosting services assist companies in establishing a presence on the internet by designing and managing internet web pages. Contracting companies can benefit from their web site by describing their services, including a "contact list" for potential clients, and by displaying photographs of their best work. Web experts advise companies to redesign their web sites at least every two to three years because old web sites can become stale and lose viewers.

A companion to a web site on the internet is the compact disk or DVD. These media are fairly inexpensive and can be designed to show off the best a company has to offer through photographs or video. Mini CDs, which are only 3 inches wide, can be easily inserted into an envelope or sent with a proposal.

Dollar Stretcher

Advertising in the telephone directory can be very expensive for a new business. One way to save money is to list your company's web site address in the directory rather than purchase a display ad. Web sites can be updated quickly while directory advertising remains the same for an entire year.

Print It!

While the internet is an incredible tool for business, many elderly citizens are not computer savvy and do not use a computer. Many others use the computer and internet for shopping and information, but not to shop for contracting services. For these folks, print advertising is a valuable tool. Costs vary depending on the type of print media used.

A simple approach is to prepare fliers that can be dropped off at individual homes; these can include some of the same information presented on the CD or can announce a special sale or discount. I know of quite a few contractors who deliver colorful and informative fliers to all the homes in the neighborhood where they are currently working.

Advertising in major metropolitan newspapers can become very expensive; local community newspapers offer better values, especially for new contractors who wish to limit their services to a small geographical area. These papers periodically print special sections that appeal to home improvement shoppers. Finally, some publishers print community magazines on a monthly basis, typically targeted to more upscale consumers. Advertising in these magazines can be fairly expensive; but your advertisements are targeted to a more affluent population.

While frequency of advertising is important—one printed advertisement is not very productive—it is not always necessary to place an expensive newspaper or magazine ad every month. One strategy is to place a full color ad every *other* month and a less expensive black and white ad during the alternate months. Most consumers do not pay close attention to when ads are placed; if they see your primary ad every other month, they will think you advertise more often. By alternating months, your advertising strategy will maintain a presence in the public eye without busting your budget.

While e-mail has become a primary means of communication, old-fashioned "snail mail," the derogatory term internet users have for mail sent by the U.S. Postal Service, has its advantages. Mailing services are very sophisticated and can target a mailing to very specific audiences based on zip code, age, gender, or income level. Sending over-sized post cards with photographs representing your work can generate new work for any company. However, in recent years it seems that the use of these large post cards is a bit over-done. I seem to receive two or three every day from a wide variety of companies. To combat this competition from mass mailers, I suggest you not only target your mailings to specific groups but also limit the message on your post card. The K.I.S.S. principle (Keep It Simple, Stupid), whose origin is in dispute, is appropriate for mailings.

Word of Mouth

By far the best, most successful, and cheapest form of marketing your company is "word of mouth." A happy client is much more likely to tell his or her friends and neighbors about the great work you've done for him than one who merely thought you did an average job. An unhappy client can do more harm to your business than nearly anything else.

Recently, a small contractor surveyed its clients and asked them which medium they were most likely to use when shopping for contracting services. "Word of mouth" was the winner by more than a two-to-one margin over telephone directories and community newspapers and magazines. The internet came in next, with radio far behind. Client surveys can be helpful in developing your business.

While small businesses usually cannot carry out indepth marketing studies, the more they know about their clients, the more chance they'll have of increasing sales. Knowing your clients' typical age, approximate income level, and personal preferences allows you to tailor your products and services to meet their particular needs.

Several techniques can be used to increase the chances that a client will give your company a good recommendation. Chapter 10 discusses relationships with clients in more detail, but from a marketing aspect the following are critical to creating and maintaining an excellent reputation:

- *Communicate with the client.* All clients appreciate knowing that their project is the most important one you are working on.

- *Present a professional image.* Employees in the field should look and dress like professionals. The best way to achieve this is to require that employees wear clean uniforms while on the job. The uniforms do not have to be fancy or expensive. Clean T-shirts with your company logo are usually acceptable, but they must be clean and well maintained. Smoking while on the job should be limited to breaks. (If you can get away with it, I suggest prohibiting all smoking during the workday.) Finally, vehicles should be well maintained, clean, and the same color. Remember the fraudulent asphalt sealers in the Preface? Their van was rusty and had no name or logo on the side; most likely it spewed black smelly exhaust as they drove off with poor Mr. Jones' money.

- *Train employees to respect your clients.* It's important that employees understand that you don't really pay their wages, the client does. While working at the jobsite, your employees should be able to answer basic questions posed by the client. If they do not know the answer to a question, they must tell the client that they don't know but will either find the answer or refer it to someone in the company who can answer it. Clients appreciate both diligence and honesty; your employees must have both.

- *Enter (and win) awards competitions.* Many contracting business associations have annual competitions that allow members to display their best work; the best are often recognized at an awards banquet. Preparing for an awards competition can be time consuming and expensive, but shortcuts cannot be taken when preparing an entry. These competitions are usually judged by a panel of your industry peers who know a substandard job when they see it. The publicity that results from winning an award is priceless because clients love doing business with companies that are among the best in their field.

Too Much of a Good Thing?

While everyone strives for success, too much of a good thing can occasionally lead to problems that overwhelm a business. Each business should strive for a professional and successful marketing and public relations campaign; but each business must also be able to meet the demands that might be generated from successful advertising. Some businesses find themselves in a situation where they are growing faster than their ability to provide quality and timely service. Anticipation of growth before it occurs will help prevent potential bottlenecks in providing goods and services to your clients. In particular, rapidly growing companies often find themselves in trouble in some or all of the following areas:

- *Lack of skilled foremen and workers.* This weakness makes it difficult to complete projects with the expected high quality.
- *Scheduling conflicts.* Most clients do not want to wait eight or ten weeks for the commencement of their project, but some fast-growing contractors make unrealistic promises for project start dates.
- *Shortage of tools and equipment needed to complete the project.* This situation often results in the purchase of equipment beyond the amount budgeted or the need to rent expensive equipment on a short-term basis.
- *Cash flow.* Can the business keep up with expenditures? Increased business usually requires an increase in outlays for materials and labor, so that the company must improve efforts to collect funds from clients.

A contracting company must understand these potential pitfalls and make contingency plans in the event that business activity grows "too fast." Rapid growth does not always follow successful marketing campaigns, but the company that fails to plan for it may become a statistic on the "business failures" list.

Chapter 8 Highlights

- ✶ Marketing is any activity that connects producers with consumers.
- ✶ Self-promotion is an excellent and inexpensive way to advertise your business.
- ✶ Every company should have some presence on the internet.
- ✶ Print advertising, while potentially expensive, can be targeted to your preferred audience.

★ Word of mouth is the number-one way most contracting companies find new clients.

★ Understanding the potential pitfalls of extremely rapid growth makes good businesss sense.

Get a Job

As a contracting business grows, it is necessary to hire employees to assist in the many tasks of operating the business. Managing employees is one of the most difficult tasks any business owner faces. Contracting companies often face additional challenges because some sectors of the industry are seasonal and some specialties have a higher turnover rate than average.

> *"It's not what you pay a man, but what he costs you that counts."*
>
> —Humorist Will Rogers (1879–1935)

Hiring and managing employees is a time-consuming task that is part psychology, part economics, and part organization. Attention to detail is required, not only for government and insurance reporting, but also because employees will descend on the payroll department if they think there is even a small error in their paycheck.

In spite of the headaches, hiring employees can be an extremely positive experience. Not only do they help the business grow and prosper, each employee also makes contributions to the personality of the company. When interviewing prospective employees, keep in mind the effect he or she will have on the mood and temperament of you, your business, and other employees.

The Employee Handbook

An employee handbook is a great tool for both employer and employee. As a company grows, it needs to create an employee handbook to document the employer's expectations of employees. The handbook will describe expected performance, how an employee can earn a raise or promotion, what fringe benefits are available, and other information such as work hours, dress code, and acceptable behavior. Owners can become better managers by participating in the process of creating the handbook because it will help them decide which policies are most important and most practical for their company. In small companies where owners and staff are not adversaries but are team members, the handbook can be a positive tool for improving morale and communications.

Both books and internet web sites provide information about creating a handbook. In addition, it is usually wise to have your lawyer take a look at the document to ensure that you are not violating state or federal law.

Most contractor handbooks include at least the following items:

- Overview of your company
- Equal opportunity statement indicating that your hiring policies are non-discriminatory
- Hours of work, lunch, and other breaks
- Wages and benefits, vacation and holiday pay
- Retirement plan rules and eligibility

- Safety policies and requirements
- Dress code
- Employment-at-will statement that says that employment can be terminated by the employer at any time for any reason
- Standards of conduct, policy on sexual harassment, smoking, alcohol use, disciplinary procedures
- Drug testing policies
- Statement that the handbook is not a contract and that policies can be changed at any time
- Signature line for employee to acknowledge that they have read and understand the handbook

It is a good idea to post a copy of the handbook near the time clock or somewhere visible to all employees. Whenever the handbook is updated, a written summary of the changes should be given to each employee.

Applications and Hiring Forms

Job applications should be straightforward and easy for the prospective employee to complete. In addition to basic contact information, the application should ask for driver's license number, level of education, special skills, and have space to list several business references. It is illegal to ask questions about race, gender, and age because these might lead to discrimination questions. Some states require that applicants fill out a special form that allows the employer to obtain detailed information about the applicant's motor vehicle record. A simple telephone call to verify references is essential. Some states provide public court records on the internet where employers can learn if an applicant has a criminal record.

Once hired, new employees must fill out Form I-9, Employment Eligibility Verification, which proves that he or she is legally permitted to work in the United States, and Form W-4, which provides the employee's social security number and indicates the allowances (deductions) she or he is claiming for income tax purposes.

Job Descriptions

Employers are also encouraged to develop written job descriptions for each job category in the company. These descriptions are useful not only to inform applicants about the job they are applying for, but can also be used during the periodic employee review. Small businesses should conduct a review with each employee at

▲

least once per year to discuss overall performance and strategies for improvement. Employers should also seek suggestions about how to improve the way the company operates.

Written job descriptions must be more than a simple list of tasks to be performed; they should be results oriented by including desired outcomes of the job. The description should start with a job purpose, which is a general summary of the job, and then include the essential functions of the job. These summarize what the employee does to complete his or her specific tasks and includes sections related to the results of these tasks. Following are several examples of items that may be included in the results-oriented portion of the job description:

- Keeps equipment operating by following operating instructions; troubleshoots breakdowns; maintains supplies; performs preventative maintenance; schedules repairs.
- Maintains a safe and secure work place by adhering to company standards and policies and to legal regulations.
- Contributes to company success by being respectful of clients and by helping other employees accomplish their tasks.

Minors Are Major

A major concern of many contracting companies is the hiring of minor employees, those under 18 years of age. Most states require that minor employees obtain a work permit prior to beginning a job. Depending upon their age, minors may be prevented from operating most power tools, driving company-owned vehicles, and assisting in "dangerous" work. The federal government has issued regulations covering the maximum hours a minor may work, both by the day and by the week. The United States Department of Labor has links to more detailed information on its web site which can be found at www.dol.gov.

Wages and Benefits

Many owners of contracting businesses will, when asked, tell you that "I probably work for about fifty cents an hour," While untrue, it sometime feels like it. On the other hand, most employees choose a job because they think that they will like the work *and* for the money. A positive workplace with caring bosses does a lot to create a successful work environment, but competitive wages and benefits are what maintain the success. Most segments of the contracting industry are unique in that the workplace changes from day to day or week to week. Workers who choose to work for contractors enjoy the variety of jobs they perform as well as the prospect of working outdoors and/or working at different locations. While some factory jobs may offer higher wages, the typical successful contracting employee would go crazy with the daily routine often found in a factory.

Many industry associations conduct periodic wage and benefit surveys and share the results with the participating companies. Contractors that take advantage of this opportunity can become more competitive because they know what their competitors are paying on average for wages and benefits; knowledge of typical wages and benefits is also useful because employers can prove to their own employees that they are keeping pace with the industry.

While benefits may be seen as the icing on the cake, most employees expect them. Employers who fail to offer these benefits will likely suffer higher turnover and have a less skilled and dedicated work force. Typically, however, most employers institute a probationary period of several months before an employee is eligible for benefits. It makes little sense to give a new employee a paid day off after working for only a few weeks.

- *Paid holidays are expected by all employees.* Typically six holidays are covered, but some employers include the day after Thanksgiving.
- *Paid vacations, based on years of service, are another expected benefit.* Seasonal contractors may wish to take into account the fact that many of their employees may be on layoff for several months.
- *Retirement plans, while not yet universal, are becoming more popular each year.* The problems faced by our social security system make it imperative that all workers take steps to prepare for retirement. Larger companies can offer a 401(k) plan giving their employees the opportunity to invest pre-tax wages that will grow tax free; the employer may make contributions to employees' accounts as well. New for 2006 is a Roth 401(k) that invests after-tax wages. These plans may be expensive and somewhat complicated to administer. Small contractors have another option called the "SIMPLE IRA." As the name implies, this plan is much easier to administer and is inexpensive for the employer. Unlike the 401(k), however, employers must make contributions to each employee's account.

Smart Tip

Employees who violate company rules or policies should receive a written warning explaining the error and what will happen to the employee if the error is repeated. By maintaining a written paper trail of policy violations, an employer both protects himself from future legal action initiated by a disgruntled employee and gives the employer ammunition when a troublesome employee demands a pay raise.

- *Use of a company vehicle, if offered, requires tedious record-keeping, especially if the employee uses the vehicle for personal use.* The value of the personal use must be included in the employee's taxable income. The rules and regulations established by the federal government are very complicated. The decision to offer this benefit should be made only after consultation with your lawyer and accountant.

- *Raises are not actually a benefit, but employers should have a policy in place regarding wage and salary raises.* Most contractors give raises once per year, after the annual employee review and when merited during the year on a case-by-case basis. Any employee promoted to a more responsible position should receive a raise, as should newer employees whose progress is above and beyond expectations. While most employers do not share wage rates among employees, employees certainly know what others make.

- *Incentive plans offer an employer a creative way to reward productive and successful employees.* While bonuses paid annually based on increases in sales or profits are a fine way to reward employees, it can be more valuable to give the bonus closer to the time when it was earned. Some companies reward employees

Dollar Stretcher

Worker's compensation rates for contracting companies are typically very high due to the risks associated with the tasks performed. While the rates are established by a government controlled bureau, the insurance companies that provide coverage offer a variety of incentive plans in which companies with good safety records receive part of their premiums back. As these rebates can be upwards of 50 percent of the total premium for large companies, an excellent incentive to promote safety is to share a portion of the rebate with safe employees. By implementing a safety contest that rewards safe employees, an employer can reduce the number of claims, which will ultimately result in high rebates. However, it should be noted that employees cannot be penalized for injuries and are required by law to report them to the employer.

immediately after a successful project is completed or pay out bonuses on a monthly basis. The most successful incentive plans reward individual effort on a continuing basis as well as companywide success on an annual basis. Much more difficult to implement is a program that penalizes serious mistakes or errors; if employees to not share in the negative results of an error, there is little incentive to avoid repeating the mistake. Ultimately, the owners of the company pay the price through reduced profits when mistakes and errors are allowed to continue.

- *Helping employees pay for continuing education can reap rewards for employers.* Technical colleges offer courses that improve the abilities of employees and do not conflict with the workday. Some associations offer certification classes where employees can learn more about their jobs and their industry. In both of these cases, the employer can assist with tuition and fees. By advertising the accomplishments of their employees, contracting businesses can both honor their employees and attract a more affluent clientele.

Turnover

"A good manager doesn't try to eliminate conflict; he tries to keep it from wasting the energies of his people. If you're the boss and your people fight you openly when they think that you are wrong—that's healthy."

—ROBERT TOWNSEND

Many companies in the contracting industry are victims of higher-than-average rates of employee turnover. Training new employees is a time-consuming and expensive undertaking, so it makes good business sense to try to hold onto your best employees. Providing a competitive wage and benefit package helps reduce turnover, but is not the only way to retain employees. Another factor that rates very highly with laborers is an enjoyable work environment where employees feel that they are part of a team and are respected and appreciated by their bosses as well as peers. Bosses who have an open door policy that gives all employees the opportunity to speak personally with the owners of the company are usually more respected than authoritarian bosses who intimidate their employees. Happy employees who work under a competitive compensation package are much more productive than employees who are constantly grumbling about the poor working conditions they are forced to work under.

An often overlooked managerial technique is simply listening to employees. New ideas often come from subordinates because they are the ones actually performing the tasks of the business. Owners and managers who encourage employees to make suggestions to improve the company help to create an atmosphere where employees feel both needed and important.

Stat Fact

Unsure about the value of incentives? Think again. Consumers are bombarded daily through newspaper advertising and mass mailings with offers from merchants for "buy one get one free," "no payments for 12 months!" and "save 50 percent with coupon." Have you ever purchased a new vehicle and borrowed the money at no interest? Or used a credit card to earn frequent flier miles? It's a fact that incentives alter behavior. The trick for employers is to find the incentives that offer the biggest reward to the company at the least cost.

Payroll Facts

According to the National Federation of Independent Business, more than 64 percent of small businesses prepare their own payrolls, about 19 percent hire a company that specializes in payroll processing, and the rest use an outside accountant or bookkeeper. As a company grows, it is more likely to employ an outside payroll service.

Not quite one half of small businesses pay their employees every week, and one quarter pay every other week.

Surprisingly, more than one half of small businesses still make out their payroll checks manually instead of using computer technology.

Not only can a company benefit financially from new ideas, but the costs of turnover can be reduced because employees feel happy that they are contributing to success.

Organizational Chart

Creating an informal organizational chart will improve communication and, in turn, the efficiency of your office. Productivity increases when each department within a company understands not only its own responsibilities but also the duties and responsibilities of other departments. To use an old cliché, "the right hand must know what the left is doing."

An organizational chart improves on both job descriptions and the company handbook because it explains the relationship between managers and subordinates. The primary aim of an organizational chart is not to define the pecking order within the organization but to indicate the decision-making structure of the company.

Many contracting businesses are overwhelmed by paperwork. On any one project some or all of the following items may be needed:

- Contract for design work
- Formal design
- Design revision
- Cost estimate
- Contract/proposal for work to be done
- Work schedule

- Work order for crew
- Inventory/order materials
- Change orders
- Subcontractor contract
- Bills from suppliers
- Profit/loss analysis
- Employee incentive payments
- Invoice sent to client
- Payment to suppliers and subcontractors
- Receipt from client
- Bank deposit
- Bank account reconciliation

Since it is highly unlikely that one department or one employee is responsible for all these tasks, it is paramount that each employee who handles a task understands who is responsible for the other tasks. Knowing the sequence of events and ensuring the proper flow of paperwork is the key to an efficient and productive office. Because it is quite common to make changes during the course of a construction project, all employees must learn to maintain an excellent paper trail of these changes. Mistakes once made are often hard to find, and if found, may be difficult to correct. A team approach to organizing and operating your company promotes efficiency and productivity, reduces errors, and creates a more functional organization.

Chapter 9 Highlights

- ★ Managing employees can be a difficult and time-consuming endeavor.
- ★ Writing an employee handbook is a great tool for both employer and employee.
- ★ Both state and federal governments have rules and regulations regarding employment; understanding and following the rules will make an owner's job easier.
- ★ Written job descriptions help employees understand their responsibilities and assist employers when reviewing employee performance.
- ★ Caution when hiring minors: stiff penalties apply if laws are violated.
- ★ Wages are important, but benefits and incentives are vitally important to employee production.
- ★ Reducing employee turnover saves money and increases productivity.
- ★ An organizational chart is an excellent tool for improving communication.

Errors and
Omissions

Typically, successful entrepreneurs are eternal optimists. When presented with a challenge, they generally attack the problem without becoming discouraged. In fact, many consider difficult circumstances as opportunities rather than setbacks; a minor detour instead of a train wreck. An excellent example of this is an excerpt from the movie *Apollo 13* (1995), which is based on the true story of the ill-fated manned mission to the moon:

NASA Director: *"This could be the worst disaster NASA's ever faced."*

Flight Director Gene Kranz: *"With all due respect, sir, I believe this is gonna be our finest hour."*

Failure Is Not an Option

The exact number of business failures among contracting companies is difficult to quantify, and it is even more difficult to know the reasons for failure. In fact, some business shutdowns may not even be classified as failures. In some cases the owner retires or sells his enterprise to another business. However, a general consensus is that roughly one half of all contracting businesses fail to survive more than five years. Once they reach the five-year anniversary, however, chances for continued success are very high.

There isn't one single overriding reason why contracting businesses fail, but failures generally fall into several categories. I've touched on some in the course of this book, but it is a worthwhile exercise to review them. Most often, failure is not caused by a single factor but by several problems working together to sink a company. Among the most prevalent causes for business failures (listed in order of occurrence) are:

- *Very rapid growth not accompanied by a like increase in resources.* If a business expands too quickly, it often cannot keep up with demand. Quality of work suffers because inexperienced or unskilled workers are hired and put to work with little or no training. Shortages of equipment also plague companies that grow too fast; when several work crews must share one piece of equipment, productivity and efficiency suffer, along with chances for profit.

- *Accounting issues.* Improper budgeting and estimating, lack of cost controls, poor cash flow, and inadequate project management spell doom for many new businesses. Contractors must have more than creativity and technical skills to succeed in the competitive contracting environment.

- *Poor oversight and control at the upper management and project management levels.* When key staffers leave the company, they are often replaced by personnel who are either incapable of doing the work or are poorly trained. When the general economy is doing very well, the pool of skilled laborers shrinks, placing more strain on newer businesses.

- *Other factors beyond the control of the owner.* Economic downturns, high inflation, shortages of materials, or the dreaded "client from hell" can cause serious damage even when a contracting business seems to be running smoothly.

On the other hand, successful contractors share many similar characteristics. While there is no single formula for success, good contractors combine most of the following assets to establish an environment where success is expected, and usually achieved:

- Good training for new employees
- Competitive wages and benefits with excellent incentives
- Low employee turnover
- Excellent management of financial resources and cash flow
- Cost controls
- Accurate job estimating
- Happy customers
- Hands-on project management
- Manageable debt
- Ability of owners and managers to identify potential problems before they get out of hand
- A cohesive and reasonable business plan

Client Complaints

Understanding exactly what angers clients the most about contractors and their services is an invaluable tool for owners. There are many resources available for owners to learn about the nature of client complaints. When a contractor understands the nature of a client, she is in a position to implement procedures to prevent trouble spots in the property development process.

Substandard workmanship is near the top of the list of client complaints. Clients expect the companies they hire to be skilled professionals, so if the work performed is unsatisfactory, trouble is right around the corner. Therefore, it is paramount that contractors properly train their employees and implement a good quality control plan.

Often, contractors work inside a client's home, disrupting normal family life. These

Tip...

Smart Tip

Understanding how clients feel about your services is critical to success. One simple technique is to insert a short questionnaire with monthly invoices. Clients can rate the quality of your work, make written comments, and even request additional services. Making operational changes based on client input will not only help retain current clients, but will assist both sales and marketing efforts.

clients prepare for the "invasion" and become very agitated if the work does not begin as promised or takes much longer to complete than expected. Contractors can make life easier for all if they implement a reasonable scheduling system and teach their employees to be respectful of the client.

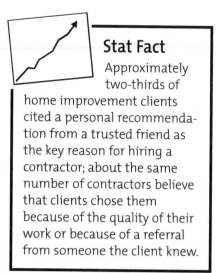

Stat Fact

Approximately two-thirds of home improvement clients cited a personal recommendation from a trusted friend as the key reason for hiring a contractor; about the same number of contractors believe that clients chose them because of the quality of their work or because of a referral from someone the client knew.

Little angers a client more than a contractor increasing the price of the project after work has been started. To avoid this problem, contractors must plan projects accurately so that all needed materials are accounted for. Designing a precise and accurate estimating system reduces errors as well. When it becomes necessary to make changes, the client must be informed in writing and must agree to both the physical alterations as well as changes in the cost of the project.

Most clients consider their homes to be their castles and are very proud of their ownership. Therefore, many of them become extremely upset when contractors do not clean up the job site both during the project and when work is completed. Failure to clean up a job site on a daily basis can give the client an impression that the contractor is performing shoddy work and does not take pride in what he does. While many people mention first impressions as an important factor when evaluating someone, the truth of the matter is that the final impression a contractor leaves when he or she finally departs the job site is more likely to be the dominant and lasting impression.

Clients pose all sorts of questions when choosing a contractor. Smart consumers talk to several contractors before engaging one to perform work. Contractors should be able to answer the following questions in a very timely manner. It should be noted, however, that clients appreciate it when a contractor or salesperson informs them that they do not know the answer but will get it within a day or two. Honesty is always the best policy. Be ready to answer:

- Are you licensed or registered in this state?
- Do you have adequate insurance coverage to protect my property and your employees?
- What other projects are you currently working on? (How's your schedule?)
- Can you provide references? I'd like to see some of the work you've done that is similar to the work I'm having done.
- Is your bid based on the same specifications as other bids?
- Do I need a building permit?
- Once you start on my project, will you stay on the job until it is completed?

- Do I have to make a decision right now? (The answer is *always* no.)
- Will you give me a written contract for the work you propose to do? (The answer is *always* yes.)

The Nightmare Client

While it is easy to find information and advice for consumers, much less is written about problem clients and how to deal with them. Some contractor associations offer advice, often through presentations at annual conferences, about dealing with the problem client. When asked, most contractors will answer:

I do not like clients who

- continually ask for work to be redone, or continually change their minds.
- constantly complain and nitpick.
- don't pay on time, think you are their banker.
- try to get you to do more work at no additional charge.
- talk too much or watch you all the time.

Sometimes a contractor realizes that a potential client has a good chance to fall into the nightmare category. In this case, honesty is a good policy. Don't be afraid to say to the potential client, "No thank you, we cannot do the work for you." However some contractors simply raise their price in hopes that the client will hire someone else. The risks in this approach is that the unwanted client will agree to your price or you get the reputation that your prices are too high.

Choose Carefully

When business is slow or the outlook for the economy as a whole is poor, competition among contractors can become intense. Competitors may drop their prices to levels below your break-even point. An old hand once commented, "Well, I'll take on some of these jobs because I can make it up on volume." Hogwash! It is silly to chase after these jobs because money lost on a project is gone forever. Another risk is actually agreeing to work for a nightmare client at a price just a few percentage points over your break-even point. Working with bad clients during tough times substantially increases the risk of losing money and certainly will result in anguish and unhappiness.

▲

How to Handle Client Complaints

Few contracting jobs are 100 percent trouble free. Many times the problem, such as a weather delay, is not the fault of the contractor. However, all complaints must be addressed and dealt with. The best rule of thumb is to approach every complaint with the attitude that the customer is always right. There is a national department store that has accepted merchandise returns for products it does not even sell!

This approach does not always result in a finding that the contractor is at fault. However, problem resolution must be the highest priority for a contracting company. Clients appreciate it when a contractor works with them instead of against them to resolve a dispute or misunderstanding. The following guidelines will help resolve complaints:

- Be courteous and listen carefully to what the client has to say.
- Don't argue with the client.
- Do not make excuses.
- Resolve problems quickly.
- Remember the importance of good client relationships.
- Be reasonable even when the problem may not be your fault.
- Make written notes of discussions.

The ultimate goal should be to resolve disputes quickly and to the satisfaction of both parties. Contractors who stand behind their work even when they are not at fault reap huge rewards over the long term. Reputations are made by happy clients. This is

Customers Can Help

TQM, or total quality management, is an approach to management that seeks to improve the quality of products and services by modifying services based on input from customers. The TQM process can be divided into four distinct categories: plan, do, check, and act. The first step is to gather data about a problem area, the second is to develop and implement a solution, the third is to verify the results by comparing before and after data, and the final step documents results and makes changes.

TQM was first used at manufacturing companies, but is currently used in a wide variety of industries, including contracting.

not to say that a contractor should back down to the client's demand on each and every issue, but he must decide which battle is really worth fighting. If the marginal cost of resolving a problem is less than the expected long-term benefit, it makes good sense to spend the time or money to satisfy the client.

Reliable Suppliers

The best run businesses can be severely hurt by unreliable suppliers or subcontractors. When an entrepreneur has built a solid team, marketed its services successfully, implemented sound financial planning procedures, and hired skilled and dedicated employees, he or she should be on the road to success. However, an efficient operation can become derailed if the materials needed to complete projects are not available when promised. The same is true when working with subcontractors: they must be reliable and complete their portion of the project both on time and within budget.

The best way to avoid problems with suppliers and subcontractors is to have an excellent communication system in place. While fax machines and e-mail can facilitate the ordering process, I recommend that new business owners personally meet with their suppliers' representatives. By getting to know your salesperson, you'll be able to shortcut problems or bottlenecks and avoid unnecessary delays in the implementation of projects.

The old adage, "You get what you pay for" is often very true when considering which supplier to use or which subcontractor to hire. While your own work force might be top notch, your image will likely suffer if the materials or subcontractors you use are below average.

Know the Enemy

"Competition is what kept me playing the psychological warfare of matching skill against skill, wit against wit."

—LOU BROCK, HALL OF FAME BASE STEALER FOR THE ST. LOUIS CARDINALS

Competition is good not only for the national economy but also for business. It forces business to eliminate waste and improve efficiency. The lifeblood of our free market, it rewards the most skilled businesses and weeds out the most inefficient. When poorly run businesses cease operations, consumers benefit because the overall quality of products and services improves; surviving businesses benefit because poorly run businesses place a drag on the entire industry, and once they are gone, its image can improve. Successful companies are forced to maintain a high level of service by improving their services or products because they must offer value to consumers that is equal or better than the competition.

It is fairly easy to enter the contracting industry, but much harder to rise above the crowd and dominate the market. One result of the relative ease of entry into contracting is that a segment of the industry is poorly managed, and a few bad apples can spoil the whole bushel.

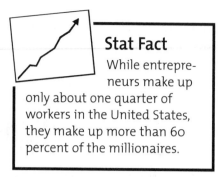

Stat Fact
While entrepreneurs make up only about one quarter of workers in the United States, they make up more than 60 percent of the millionaires.

While some industries, and I'm sure you can name a few, have chronically poor reputations, a few others are always held in high regard, and the largest segment has a mixture. Contractors fall into this huge middle.

Each entrepreneur should look at competition as a way to improve his organization's performance and success. Success is achieved by gathering better information about customers and new products than your competition, using the information for making the best choices for your organization, and finally, turning the choices made into actions that will provide a competitive advantage.

Never fear the competition. Never speak badly about the competition publicly. Just beat the competition with a better business plan, better financial management, better services and products, and with competitive pricing.

An excellent way to use your competition to your own benefit is to join your local or regional industry association. Many of these schedule monthly meetings where members meet for dinner and listen to a speaker. It's not only an excellent time to learn about new initiatives in the industry but also a very good time to network with other owners and learn about their problems and successes. Supplier members usually attend these functions and can provide insight into new products or methods of installation. Associations also offer educational seminars during the year for both the business owner and key employees.

Employers who stand still, never changing their methods of operation, will eventually get run over by their competition. Skilled entrepreneurs are constantly on the alert for ways to improve all facets of their business. They *use* competition to improve their skills and help develop products and services that consumers value highly.

Hiring Subcontractors

In this era of specialization, the use of subcontractors has become very common. While there are many benefits to hiring a specialist to complete a portion of a property development project, caution is necessary. If the subcontractor is unqualified, the problems obviously offset the benefits. When hiring several subcontractors, the general contractor must have the ability to coordinate the work of the various subcontractors. In most projects, establishing a proper sequence of work is critical to success. The general contractor who hires the subcontractors must understand the responsibilities of each sub and how each fits into the overall construction sequence. For example, it is no use to schedule the asphalt contractor to install the driveway if the excavating contractor has not completed the rough grading.

Of foremost importance is hiring a subcontractor who is extremely reliable and able to meet the schedule established for the project. Because timing is usually crucial to a successful project, subcontractors must be able to complete their work in a timely manner. And because the best subcontractors are usually in great demand, a general contractor cannot risk losing the services of one sub because of the inefficiency of another. In addition, subcontractors must be able to meet the quality standards of the project set by the client, architect, and general contractor. While high quality work is always expected of subcontractors, high-end projects with large budgets demand more skill and detail than low-budget projects. Subcontractors must understand what is expected of them and set their schedules accordingly.

An often overlooked detail in hiring a subcontractor is insurance. When hiring a sub, the general contractor should be sure that the sub has proper insurance. While general liability insurance is very important, especially to protect against a lawsuit, carrying workers' compensation insurance is critical. Insurance companies usually audit their clients each year; during the audit, they verify that all subcontractors carry workers' compensation insurance. If they do not, then the general contractor will be charged an amount as if the subcontractors were its own employees. It is not unusual for a general contractor to add only 5 to 15 percent of the subcontractor's fee to the client's cost of the project, so an unexpected charge for workers' compensation insurance would nearly erase the profit generated by the subcontractor's work.

Chapter 10 Highlights

★ Approximately 50 percent of new businesses fail to survive five years; however once the fifth anniversary is reached, success is likely.

★ The primary complaint that clients have about contractors is substandard workmanship. Therefore, it is critical to hire quality employees and implement a good training program.

★ Learn to recognize the warning signs of nightmare clients, and either decline to work for them or take extra precautions when preparing for the work.

★ Because few projects are completely trouble free, learn how to handle client complaints in an understanding and professional manner.

★ Reliable suppliers are extremely valuable.

★ Competition can be very good for the best contractors.

★ Hiring subcontractors can be beneficial, but care must be taken to hire the most reliable.

★ Attention to detail is critical when working with clients, suppliers, and subcontractors.

PANIC
Is Proper

Well, here we are at the final chapter, nearly ready to say goodbye. But instead of reaching an end, I hope this book will lead to a new beginning for you. While starting and running your own contracting business presents innumerable challenges and obstacles, the potential rewards, both personal and financial, far outweigh them. This chapter puts it all together, highlighting key points presented in the previous chapters.

"Getting ahead in a difficult profession requires avid faith in yourself. That is why some people with mediocre talent, but with great inner drive, go so much further than people with vastly superior talent."

—Academy Award-winning Italian actress, Sophia Loren

When to PANIC

Often the daily life of a contractor is chaotic and messy. Schedules are disrupted by weather and absent employees. Projects are delayed because supplies are not available as promised. Clients call with change orders and seemingly inane concerns. Vendors call asking when payment will be made for merchandise. An employee thinks that his paycheck is incorrect. The computer crashes. A truck has a flat tire. Two work crews need the same piece of equipment. And your children are home from school because they have the flu and your spouse has to tend to an ailing parent.

While many people would cower in fear or become completely unglued with crises, ending up reclining on a psychiatrist's couch, successful contractors and entrepreneurs thrive on activity, variety, and challenge. They are able to step back from daily chaos and view the big picture, understand where it is all leading, and forge ahead with the business of their business.

While successful contractors do not panic during challenging times, there are reasons why small business owners should PANIC in order to be successful. While not inclusive or unique, my PANIC list gives the important factors required to become a thriving and happy contractor.

Astute readers will notice that I do not mention high intelligence or IQ, nor do I include advanced degrees. Intelligence and education are important, but they are not the most important aspect of becoming a successful contractor. Contractors are practical folks with unique talents that cannot be measured by university degrees and advanced placement testing. Sure they might have to pass competency tests in their home state, but these are usually practical exercises devised by politicians attempting to protect the public.

Let's PANIC Now

Of course, entrepreneurs should not actually panic when events take a wrong turn; just remember that failure is not an option. However, after reading the remainder of the chapter you'll understand that my definition of PANIC cannot be found in any dictionary.

P is for Perseverance

Successful contractors exhibit steady persistence in spite of the many obstacles that they meet each day. Running a business is a difficult, sometimes discouraging undertaking. Entrepreneurs are able to look to the distant future, stick with their long-range plan, and not get sidetracked by temporary difficulties. In recent years, we have seen several high-tech companies with business plans that include losing money for a number of years. They knew they would lose money but still stayed the course and ultimately became profitable. Perseverance implies a great deal of optimism about the future and a strong passion for your work. If you really believe in the future and believe that your work is important to your community, you'll be able to overcome adversity, win clients, and own a respected, profitable, and successful business. And as my favorite actress said, having faith in yourself allows you to go further than others and rise to the top of your profession.

A is for Accounting

A good sense of financial management is critical to succeeding as an entrepreneur. Because cash flow is usually a concern for those in the contracting industry, timely management of cash inflows and expenses often makes the difference between a successful business and one that ultimately fails. In many parts of the country, contractors have to contend with seasonal fluctuations of income and expenses, which makes long-range financial planning essential for success. Successful contractors establish a reasonable budget, use it to implement a competitive system for establishing prices, and regularly monitor both income and expenses to ensure that their financial management plan is on track.

Read and re-read Chapters 6 and 7 until you have an excellent understanding of the

Tip...

Smart Tip

I know of a landscape contractor who works in the northern part of the country. Typically, he has to lay off the majority of his employees for three months during the winter months. Income drops to a trickle, but fixed costs remain to be paid. Before any bonuses are paid to key executives, he ensures that enough cash is on hand to tide the company through the lean months. As one of owners told us, "In the winter it often seems like we dig a big hole in the ground and throw money into it." He also has a mathematical formula for distributing bonuses that ensures there are funds available to reinvest in the company as it grows. Not only is the company able to purchase new equipment, it keeps its interest expenses at a manageable level.

relationship between income and the various expense categories. In addition, complete understanding of contribution margin is a key piece of knowledge for contractors. Mathematics scares lots of people, but with perseverance anyone can learn the basic techniques of budgeting and estimating.

Starting your own contracting business involves a certain amount of risk because of the degree of competition in the industry and because many specialty contractors require a substantial financial investment just to get started. However, the risks can be greatly reduced by employing a sound and consistent financial plan.

N is for Natural Ability

In general, contractors are creative craftspeople who use their innate skills to develop their business. Creativity comes in many forms: Some have the power of visualization and can "see" how the many elements of a project fit together. Others are masters of scale and proportion who can place individual elements together. Yet others are true artists who can make perfect individual elements that fit into the whole. Many have an excellent aesthetic sense and make creations that have good taste and a sense of beauty. Finally, successful contractors understand that many times "form follows function" and use their skills to ensure that their creations not only look appropriate for their task but also "work." Whatever form or forms of creativity these entrepreneurs display, they all have full confidence in their own natural abilities. This self-confidence allows them to forge ahead and take on the risks that are inherent in starting a new business.

College Drop-Outs

While I applaud those who aspire to higher education and do not recommend dropping out of college, several famous entrepreneurs actually did drop out of college (or took a leave of absence) to pursue their dreams. Their natural abilities and creativity allowed them to succeed without completing their formal education. Here's a short list of well-known names with the company they founded and the college they attended: Bill Gates, Microsoft, Harvard; Michael Dell, Dell Computer, University of Texas; Steve Jobs, Apple Inc, Reed College; and Paul Allen, Microsoft, Washington State University.

At the other end of the spectrum, Google Inc.'s founders Larry Page and Sergey Bin both received Master's degrees from Stanford; I understand that Bin's plans for earning a Ph.D. from Stanford are currently on hold while he works at Google.

Natural ability and creativity are not limited to merely the physical aspect of a contractor's work. Creative accounting can save a contracting company thousands of dollars each year without risking the intrusion of the Internal Revenue Service. Creative use of employee incentives can raise the level and quality of the work produced by the company. Every aspect of managing a contracting business can benefit from creative thought, and the most successful entrepreneurs tap into their own natural abilities and, at the same time, know how to release the creativity of the people who work around them.

In addition, contractor-owners must be able to multitask, that is, understand, recognize, and react to all that is happening around them—not only to the day-to-day events of running the business but also to the consequences of many conflicting personalities working together for a common goal. On the other hand, owners must be able to focus on the immediate task at hand and avoid getting sidetracked on unimportant issues.

I is for Instinct

Most of the skills required to operate a successful contracting business can be learned, either through formal training or from experience. However, instinct, which really means having a good feel for business, is something that cannot be taught. It is the intangible something that separates the most successful entrepreneurs from the average business owner. Those with good instincts really know themselves and, most importantly, understand their own strengths and weaknesses, turn this knowledge into an asset, and create an efficient and profitable entity. These folks not only have the ability to talk a good game, they can also execute their plans to the benefit of the company.

Business owners who really understand themselves also understand their own shortcomings and take steps to balance their weaknesses by surrounding themselves with people who compensate for then. The best and most successful realize that their success is often a result of the people around them rather than themselves alone. Instinct, or good business sense, allows these entrepreneurs to get the most out of the people around them and build a true team with a common goal.

Confidence is an asset, arrogance a liability.

C is for Communication

Excellent communication skills make up the final section of the reasons to PANIC. Communicating is less about making stirring speeches than it is about the ability to convey enthusiasm and energy to both employees and clients. With the emergence of the internet, e-mail, cellular telephones, and voice mail, our lives have become more impersonal than at any time in recent memory. Thus, in the modern world, possessing good people skills is of greater importance to the entrepreneur. Not only must the contractor be able to accurately share his or her corporate vision to fellow workers but he or she must also be able to convey enthusiasm, professionalism, and sincerity to clients.

Communicating with employees starts with hiring the right people for the job; some of the smartest people in the business world are extremely dumb when it comes to hiring employees. Good hiring is a result of being able to put yourself in another person's shoes and see what they see, feel what they feel, and have sensitivity to their expectations. Upon hiring the right people, good communication means having the ability to motivate the new employees to succeed beyond their dreams, pushing them to their creative limits, and then recognizing their achievements.

Communicating with clients follows a similar path. The ability to sell your service or product requires that you be able to sit in their chairs, understand their problems, and focus on their dreams. When you have faith in yourself and your natural abilities, you'll be able to communicate more successfully with clients; they will feel your excitement and catch your enthusiasm.

But, What If . . .?

Not every entrepreneur possesses all of the traits mentioned in PANIC. Not everyone is a good communicator, not all have excellent natural ability. But to succeed, you must recognize both your strengths and weaknesses. When you do this, you will have the ability to hire people who are strong in areas you are weak. The combination of talent within a company creates a stronger and more powerful entity.

Put Me in Coach

With all due respect to professional baseball, professional basketball, and NASCAR fans, most polls indicate that professional football holds the top spot as America's favorite sport. Football is a very complex business requiring the expertise of dozens of people in each organization. Gone are the days of Vince Lombardi and George Halas who controlled entire football operations with only a handful of assistants. Today, most teams separate the head coach and general manager positions, and it is not unusual to have 16 or 17 assistant coaches on the staff. The salary cap and player contracts are so complex that only a team of lawyers can understand them. All this for a team with only 45 active players.

Running a business is much like coaching a football team. The head football coach oversees both the offense and the defense; assistants manage the details of each. In order to win, both offense and defense have to play extremely well. The offense is led by the quarterback. The wide receivers and running backs attempt to advance the ball. The offensive line, tight ends, and fullback provide support. They have one and only one goal: score points. The defense, with defensive linemen, linebackers, and the backfield players, also has one goal: prevent the offense from scoring points.

The offensive squad of a business includes the marketing department, sales force, and the bidding and estimating departments. Depending on the size of the company, landing a $40,000 or $200,000 job can be compared to a quarterback throwing a long touchdown pass; but the business "offense" still needs to book $500 and $5,000 jobs, just like the offense needs to gain a few yards at a time to get a first down. For the business, the "defense" is made up of those who manage the finances of the company. If they are not successful, the game gets out of hand, and success (victory) is impossible. A football team may have an excellent offense, but if its defense is weak, it will likely lose more games than it wins.

The point of this analogy is that careful financial management is like having a really good defensive team. In fact, in many ways it is more important to have a great defense than a good offense. If you are not sure, go back and read Chapter 7, study contribution margin, and understand what the offense must do if the defense overspends the budget.

Just consider recent winners of the Super Bowl, football's world championship contest. They have almost always had the better defense. Look at most of the great teams of their day—the Packers, Steelers, Bears, Dolphins, and the 49ers; even though they had great quarterbacks like Brett Favre and Dan Marino, they also had exceptional defensive teams. And they all won lots of games—and Super Bowls.

Release all your creativity and passion with your offensive plan, but be stubborn and watchful with your defensive scheme. Teamwork wins when players on both sides of the ball do their part.

The Beginning

As my book concludes, your new life begins.

"The important thing is not being afraid to take a chance. Remember the greatest failure is to not try. Once you find something you love to do, be the best doing it."

—DEBBI FIELDS, FOUNDER OF MRS. FIELDS COOKIES

Appendix
Construction Contracting Resources

They say you can never be rich enough or young enough. While these could be argued, we believe you can never have enough resources. Therefore, we present for your consideration a wealth of sources for you to check into, check out, and harness for your own personal information blitz.

These sources are tidbits, ideas to get you started on your research. They are by no means the only sources out there, and they should not be taken as the ultimate answer. Research has been done on each company, but businesses do tend to move, change, fold, and expand. Please do your homework carefully, and then get out and start investigating.

Books and Magazines

Online book sellers
>   www.amazon.com
>   www.barnesandnoble.com
>   www.bordersstores.com
>   www.abebooks.com
>   www.bookfinder.com

Architectural Graphic Standards by Charles George Ramsey and John Ray, Jr. Hoke, (John Wiley & Son, 2000).

Common Sense Economics: What everyone should know about wealth and prosperity by James Gwartney, Richard Stroup, and Dwight Lee, (St. Martin Press, 2005).

Construction Forms and Contracts by Craig Savage and Karen Jones-Mitchell, (Craftsman Books, 1994).

Contracting in All 50 States by R.L. Bryson, (Craftsman Books, 1998).

Introduction to Type in Organizations: Individual Interpretive Guide by Sandra Krebs Hirsch and Jean M. Kummerow, (Consulting Psychologists Press, Inc., 1998).

The Only Three Questions That Count by Ken Fisher, (John Wiley & Son, 2007).

Please Understand Me II: Temperament, Character, Intelligence by David Keirsey, (Prometheus Nemesis Book Company, 1988).

Ultimate Start-Up Directory by James Stephenson, (Entrepreneur Press, 2001).

Construction, Remodeling, and General Contractor magazines www.your tradepubs.com

Government Resources

Employment information, www.eeoc.gov

General information, www.business.gov

Internal Revenue Service, 800-829-4933, www.irs.gov

Small Business Administration, 800-827-5722, www.sba.gov

U.S. Department of Labor, 866-487-2365, www.dol.gov

Worker's Compensation, www.workerscompensation.com

Business Operations

Interest rate information, www.bankrate.com

Cellular telephone information
www.wirelessguide.org
www.myrateplan.com

Contractor resources
www.contractorresources.com
www.websites4contractors.com

Accounting software
> www.peachtree.com, 877-291-8401
> www.myob-us.com, 800-322-6962
> www.quickbooks.intuit.com, 888-729-1996

Credit Rating Bureaus

Equifax
P.O. Box 740241
Atlanta, GA 30374
(800) 685-1111
Web site: www.equifax.com

Experian
P.O. Box 9554
Allen, TX 75013
(888) 397-3742
Web site: www.experian.com

Find your credit rating
Web site: www.annualcreditreport.com

TransUnion LLC
P.O. Box 1000
Chester, PA 19022
(800) 888-4213
Web site: www.transunion.com

Education/Industry Links

Colleges and universities, www.collegeboard.com

Architecture
> www.naab.org
> www.aia.org

Landscape architecture, www.asla.org

Engineering
> www.abet.org
> www.nspe.org

Design-Build Institute, www.dbia.org

Construction industry associations, www.thebluebook.com/links.html

▲

Information and Tools

Counselors to America's Small Business, www.score.org

Forbes Magazine, www.forbes.com/entrepreneurs

Tools, http://startupbiz.com

Wall Street Journal, http://startup.wsj.com

Glossary

Accrual accounting. An accounting system that recognizes revenue when earned and expenses when incurred; income and expenses are recorded at the end of an accounting period even though cash has not been received or paid.

Break-even. The point where expenses and income are equal.

Business plan. A written summary of how a business intends to organize an entrepreneurial endeavor and implement activities and procedures necessary and sufficient for the business to succeed.

CAD: Computer Aided Design. The use of a personal computer and specialized software to prepare two-dimensional drawings.

Cash accounting. An accounting method that recognizes revenue and expenses when cash is actually received or disbursed rather than when earned or incurred.

Cash flow. An accounting term that refers to the amount of cash that is received and spent by a business; it is not a measure of profitability; a profitable company can fail because of problems with cash flow.

Contribution margin. The amount of revenue available to pay fixed costs and profits after paying direct costs and variable costs.

Debt financing. A method of financing a business that relies on borrowing to fund the initial activities of the business.

Design/build. Generally, a contracting company that provides both professional design services and construction services; most often these are bundled into one package.

Direct costs. Expenses directly related to specific jobs or projects; usually includes materials, labor, and labor burden and may include the cost of equipment rental and subcontractors.

Equity financing. A method of financing an enterprise in which a company sells stock; individuals who purchase the stock have ownership claims on the business.

Fixed costs. An expense that remains constant regardless of a change in the level of a company's business or income.

Fringe benefit. Payments to employees in addition to their wage or salary; often fringe benefits are tax free to the employee.

General contractor. A contractor who constructs a building or other property improvement for a client; may have its own work force or may hire independent subcontractors.

Google. An internet company that specializes in providing free online search capabilities for computer users.

Independent contractor. A person or business that contracts to do work according to his or her own methods.

Labor burden. Costs of labor in addition to wage or salary; includes payroll taxes, insurance, and other associated expenses.

Law of unintended consequences. Philosophical theory that every action or decision results in one or more unexpected outcomes; these may be positive, negative, or neutral in their effect.

Lien. A legal claim on a piece of property used to ensure payment of a debt or obligation.

Marginalism. An economic concept used to determine if an additional expense will result in a benefit greater than the additional cost.

Marketing. Any activity that connects producers with consumers.

Mission statement. A written statement that summarizes the purpose of a business.

MSDS: Material Safety Data Sheet. An important feature of workplace safety, these sheets provide information for dealing with toxic or hazardous materials.

Businesses are required to maintain a current file of MSDS applicable to their enterprise.

MYOB. Accounting software for small business.

OJT: On the Job Training. Learning a trade or job without formal education.

OSHA: Occupational Health and Safety Administration. A branch of the federal government responsible for establishing and enforcing procedures to prevent workplace injuries.

Overhead. Fixed costs plus variable costs.

PBX: Private Branch Exchange. A computerized telephone system that can handle many calls, both incoming and outgoing, at the same time; voice mail and call forwarding are popular additional features.

Peachtree. An accounting software package for small business developed by Sage Software.

SIMPLE IRA. A company-sponsored retirement plan.

Subcontractor. A contractor hired to complete a portion of work included under another contractor's contract.

TQM: Total Quality Management. A management strategy aimed at creating awareness of quality in all organizational processes; provides a system under which everyone in the organization can strive for customer satisfaction.

QuickBooks. Popular accounting software developed by Inuit.

Variable costs. Expenses of a business that usually change in real terms, or dollar amounts, as the level of business activity increases; in addition, they tend to remain about the same *percentage* of direct costs.

Worker's compensation insurance. Insurance that is designed to protect the earnings of employees who are injured or become ill as a result of their work; premium costs are based on payroll.

Index

Internet
  access, 46
  as essential, 57
  as marketing tool, 91–92
IRS, 34–38

L

Labor burden calculation for field labor,
  Figure 6-1, 61
Labor law posters, 48–49
Lawyer, hiring a, 33
Legal structure, business, 30–32
Liens, 50
Limited liability company (LLC), 30
Lingo, learning industry, 16–17
Logos, corporate, 89–90

M

Magazines, recommended, 125–126
Management expertise, 18–19
Managing people, 19
Marketing, 89–96
Material Safety Data Sheets (MSDS), 49
Math worksheet, 80
Minor's work permit, 49, 100
Mission statement, 25–26
Money issues, 17–20
Monthly "physical exam" to monitor
  spending, 83–86

N

Newspaper column, writing a, 90–91

O

Office specifications and details, 42
Office staff and labor burden, Figure 6-3,
  65–66
Office supplies, 46
  checklist, 47–48
Office, opening your, 40–42
On-the-job (OJT) training, 11–12
Online banking, 50
OOPS factor, the, 26–27
Operating expenses, 17–18

Organization, management of your, 20
OSHA forms and regulations, 49
Outside contractors, types of, 4

P

PANIC (Perseverance, Accounting,
  Natural ability, Instinct,
  Communication), 117–121
  accounting, 119–120
  communication, 121–122
  instinct, 121
  natural ability and creativity, 120–121
  perseverance, 119
Partnership, 30
Players, the, 3–5
Press releases, 91
Profitability, financial techniques for,
  55–78
Profits
  contribution margin, the key to under-
    standing, 79–87
  the bottom line, 76–77
Promoting your services, 89–96
Property development contractor, 3
Property owner as general contractor, 4–5

R

Ratio analysis, 77
Record-keeping, 36–38
Resources, list of construction and con-
  tracting, 125–128

S

S corporation, 31
Sales per labor dollar, Figure 7-3, 86
Savings, six-month nest egg, 17
Schedule, work, 51–52
Seasonal fluctuations, weathering, 53, 119
Seeing the big picture, 51–52
Self-promotion, 90–91
Self-reliance, 13
Simple estimate, Figure 6-8, 75
Software, accounting, 57–58

▲